Mary the Mother of All

Mary the Mother of All

Protestant Perspectives
and Experiences
of Medjugorje

Edited by Sharon E. Cheston

A Campion Book

Loyola University Press
Chicago

Loyola University Press
3441 North Ashland Avenue
Chicago, Illinois 60657

Cover and interior design by Nancy Gruenke
Cover photograph by Art Zamur, Liaison International

Library of Congress Cataloging-in-Publication Data

Mary the mother of all : Protestant perspectives and experiences of
    Medjugorje / Sharon E. Cheston, editor.
        p.   cm.
    ISBN 0-8294-0775-8
    1. Christian pilgrims and pilgrimages—Bosnia and Hercegovina
—Medjugorje. 2. Mary, Blessed Virgin, Saint—Apparitions and mir-
acles—Bosnia and Hercegovina—Medjugorje. 3. Medjugorje
(Bosnia and Hercegovina)—Religious life and customs. 4.
Protestants—Religious life. 5. Mary, Blessed Virgin, Saint, and
Christian union.   I. Cheston, Sharon E.
BT660.M44M375   1994
232.91'7'0949742—dc20   94-25053
                                                                CIP

*T*o our Holy Mother who we never knew was there for us. Thank you for revealing yourself to us and to all the people of the earth.

Contents

*D*ear children . . . pray so that in prayer
you may be able to comprehend what is
God's plan through you . . .

—Message given to visionaries by Mary,
January 25, 1987

A Letter to the Reader

I t was after "prayerful consideration" that Sharon Cheston decided to edit *Mary the Mother of All: Protestant Perspectives and Experiences of Medjugorje*. That same mother smiled lovingly upon her daughter and whispered gently, "Thank you, Sharon, for having responded to my call."

Sharon set out to fulfill God's plan in early April 1991. A comparison couldn't help but be made between the similarity of her venture and the Annunciation of our Lady when Sharon wrote in a letter to me, "I do not understand why I'm being called to this, but I'll trust in God: that's how I got to go to Medjugorje in the first place" (April 4, 1991). Recalling that pilgrimage with Sharon and Jim, Shannon and Kelly, I was in complete agreement. I would describe them as an unusually spirit-filled Lutheran family whose steps never falter once convinced of truth.

A walk in faith! Blessed are those who have not seen and yet have believed (John 20:29). Blessed, indeed, is she, who, like Noah and Abraham, trusted God to keep his promise to those who obey (Hebrews 11:7–11). The fruits of hard labor, prayer, and faith are clearly seen in this book as an invisible chain that links witness to witness. While every chapter unfolds the unique story of shining light in the dark, each account is basically alike: a mother calls; a child responds and discovers the way to the truth. Mary leads her children to the source of life, Jesus, her divine son, who cries out to the Father: "Father, may they be one in us; just as You are in Me and I am in You. May they be one so that the world will believe that You sent Me" (John 17:21).

Whether people are Lutheran, Presbyterian, Unitarian, Episcopalian, Baptist, or any other denomination, all are God's children. In our Lady's own words (spoken in January 1985), she says,

It is you who are divided on Earth. The Muslim and the Orthodox, for the same reason as Catholics, are equal before my Son and me. You are all my children. Those who are not Catholics are no less creatures made in the image of God and destined to rejoin, someday in the house of the Father. Salvation is available to everyone without exception. Only those who refuse God deliberately are condemned (Two Friends of Medjugorje 1990, 123–24).

Jesus delivers a similar message, which is potrayed in the *Poem of the Man-God* (a book recommended to visionary Marija in Medjugorje by our Blessed Mother). Jesus tells his followers:

After the end of the world no other virtue will survive except Charity, that is, the Union of all the creatures who lived in justice, with the Creator. There will not be several Heavens: one for Israel, one for Christians, one for Catholics, one for Gentiles, one for heathens. There will be one Heaven only. And likewise there will be one reward only: God, the Creator, Who rejoins His creatures who lived according to justice, and in whom, because of the beauty of the souls and bodies of saints, He will admire Himself with the joy of Father and of God. There will be one Lord only. Not one Lord for Israel, one for Catholicism, one for each of the other religions (Valtorta 1989).

One common thread that unites all of those whose stories are written on these pages is their longing for peace and being drawn to the woman who comes as "our Lady, Queen of Peace." It has always been my belief that our holy desires are first God's desires stirred up in our hearts through grace. It is then up to us to choose whether or not we will pay the price necessary to obtain the desired goal. God is the initiator, like a father who attracts his child to what is good by presenting a glimmer of some *attainable* reward. A brief experience of peace in our heart whets the appetite for more. In Medjugorje, the Mother of Jesus is sent not only to attract God's children to the peace of heaven, but to show us the way. The path her son points out is the path of conversion, prayer, fasting, and faith. As each story is revealed, the reader will come to an understanding of how this path leads to peace.

In conclusion, I wish to express to God the deep joy and gratitude in my heart for the privilege of meeting people of faith in my journey through life. It is truly a hopeful sign that says to me God's Kingdom is close at hand. My prayer is twofold: First, for the reader that each heart and mind will be open to the messages of our Lady at Medjugorje that are found in this book. May all be brought to an awareness of the existence of God, the risen Jesus, Son of God, and of his return in glory one day. Second, for Sharon, the one who said yes to the possibility of giving birth to *Mary the Mother of All*. May she be blessed with an ever-increasing faith that echoes throughout her life, "Let it be according to your word."

Sister Jane Culligan, S.C.

T here is only one God, one faith. Let the people believe firmly and do not fear anything.

—Message given to visionaries by Mary, June 29, 1981

An Introduction to the Events Occurring in Medjugorje

Sharon E. Cheston

E ven though extraordinary events have transpired in Medjugorje from June 1981 to the present, many are still unaware of the spiritual occurrences that have been affecting the small town in Yugoslavia and have drawn over twenty million pilgrims from all over the world to the three small villages which make up Medjugorje. (I have heard several pronunciations of the word *Medjugorje*. However, the local townspeople say, "Med yew GOR ria.")

The small Croatian town is located in the central western part of Yugoslavia, approximately forty-five minutes west of Mostar and three hours north and east of Dubrovnik. Until recently, Medjugorje was not easy to locate on a world atlas. But in 1981 when the apparitions began, the town with a population of approximately 650 people gained the world's attention. Today the number of residents has jumped to around eleven hundred, most of whom participate in welcoming, housing, and feeding the hundreds of thousands of pilgrims each year. Although pilgrims have avoided the area since 1991 because of the severe political strife, the town continues to worship and attend to Mary's messages and teachings.

The following paragraphs briefly outline the history of the apparitions. For more complete and detailed information, please refer to Wayne Weible's book *Medjugorje: The Message,* published in 1989.

On June 24, 1981, two children were taking a walk on a rocky hillside when they saw the Madonna. Later, joined by a third teen, they were gathering some sheep when they saw the Virgin Mary standing on the hill holding Baby Jesus in her arms. They instantly recognized Mary and ran away. Taking more children back to the spot with them, they returned to

see if she was still there. She was. On June 25 she spoke to
them saying, "I have come to tell you God exists." Some children who saw Mary during the first few apparitions were not
permitted by their parents to return, but others joined the
core group. The final group of young people who continued
to have daily apparitions ranged in ages from ten to seventeen
when the apparitions began and included two boys and four
girls. Mary told the children when and where she would
appear to them, and the children told the villagers. The word
spread, and by the end of the week five thousand people were
gathering on what became known as Apparition Hill to see
Mary. Because Yugoslavia was under the rule of the Communist party, which did not embrace religion but only tolerated it
in the churches, this new spiritual phenomenon responsible
for bringing so many people was, in the eyes of the authorities, getting out of hand. Therefore, the police began barri-
cading the town's roads to keep the villagers from going to
the hills during the apparitions. The faithful, determined to
be on site for Mary's appearances, proceeded to leave the
roads and walk over the mountains. When the police saw that
they could not control the crowd, they turned to controlling
the children. The young people were arrested, threatened,
and informed that they would not be permitted to see Mary
any longer. Since the police believed that the apparition was a
hoax made up by the six children, they believed that they
could control the eventual outcome. They were particularly
interested in the youngest member of the group, Jakov, who
was only ten at the beginning of the apparitions, and considered him the one most likely to "crack" under pressure and
admit the hoax. At the same time, the village priest, Father
Jozo Zovko, was also doubting the authenticity of the apparitions. He was not sure exactly what was happening, but he did
not believe that Mary was appearing to the children. Below is
Father Jozo's story of his own personal conversion to the truth
of the apparitions, and it involves the youngest visionary.

Jakov was taken to the police station and threatened by the
police. He was told emphatically that he was not going to see
Mary again. Jakov calmly told the police that they could not
tell Gospa (the Croatian word for "our Lady") not to appear
to him. The police retorted that if Mary continued to appear

to Jakov then they would throw Jakov and his family in jail. Jakov replied, "That you *can* do, but you *cannot* tell Gospa what to do." Jakov and all the children were unshakable in their convictions. Frustrated by these brave children, the police placed Jakov and the other visionaries under house arrest. While confined to his home, Jakov was at times frightened and hid under his kitchen table behind a long tablecloth. One day while the villagers were at Mass, Gospa appeared to Jakov under the kitchen table. She told him that she wanted him to run to the church, which was a kilometer away, and tell the people that Mary said, "Pray the rosary and pray together." Jakov replied that he could not leave because he was under house arrest and there was a guard outside his door. Mary told Jakov that he should trust in God.

Jakov crept out from under the table, went to the front door, and saw that the guard had fallen asleep, so he began running quickly toward the church. The guard awoke and began chasing him, but Jakov was able to hail villagers driving cars. By changing cars several times, he evaded the police and arrived at Saint James Church. Breathless, barefoot, and determined, Jakov threw open one of the doors to the church, ran down the center aisle in the middle of the mass, and hid under the altar cloth. Father Jozo stopped mass, peered under the altar cloth, and asked Jakov what he was doing. Jakov replied that he had a message for the people, so Father Jozo (still not convinced of the apparitions' validity) lifted Jakov up and stood him on the altar so that he could state the message to all present. To this day, Father Jozo states that when he kneels to kiss the altar he can still visualize those two dirty footprints left on the altar cloth by Jakov's dusty bare feet. Jakov announced to the people that Gospa said to "pray the rosary and pray together." Father Jozo relates to pilgrims that he remembers thinking that if he were only ten years old and he was claiming to see the Virgin Mary, then he would have fabricated something as simple as that statement, too. No sooner were his doubting thoughts completed than Mary appeared in the Church in front of all those who were attending mass and said, "Pray the rosary and pray together."

A short time later Father Jozo felt called upon to protect the children by hiding them from the police. He also defied an order that banned Mass, which led to his arrest and eighteen months in jail. Upon his release from jail he was given a small church forty-five minutes from Medjugorje, and there he spoke to pilgrims, blessed them, and carried out his priestly duties. Recently, he has been reassigned but still speaks to pilgrims regularly. He is a gifted and blessed speaker who inspires everyone who hears him. While the archbishop and the parish priests believe in the authenticity of the appearance of Gospa, the previous bishop, Bishop Zanic, was not supportive and saw the situation as fabrication and manipulation by the parish priests. Oddly enough, when Bishop Zanic publicly condemned the apparitions, the police seemed to lose interest in or deemphasize the importance of the occurrences, thus enabling the children, the villagers, and the pilgrims to freely gather and worship. From then on, the apparitions continued in the church and on the hill without interference by the police. Bishop Zanic has continued to disclaim the apparitions and during his tenure made demands on the priests, villagers, and visionaries to change the place where the children see Mary. The children acceded to the demands and, except for these inconveniences, the visions continued to occur daily. The current bishop supports the authenticity of the apparitions.

The messages that Mary has been giving to the visionaries and to the world are the most significant gifts of the entire ten-year history of the apparitions. In my opinion, some of Mary's most meaningful messages are that she is the mother of all of us, she is calling all of us back to God, and she is showing us the way to achieve our conversion and return to God. When Mary speaks of conversion, she is not speaking of conversion to a particular religion but of a conversion of our hearts to God. In fact, the people of the parish of Saint James welcome all people from all religions to their church, and, while the tradition of the church is definitely Roman Catholic, I do not believe I have been in any church where I have felt a more unified ecumenical spirit. Some Protestants have mentioned that, at first, the Roman Catholic atmosphere and rituals are too overbearing. After a few days, however, they agree that the honest, welcoming, inclusive, loving atmosphere erodes the differences between religions and distills the purity of faith. It is difficult to explain or imagine unless you have been there in person, but as you read each person's story in the following chapters, you will see the power of Medjugorje's welcoming atmosphere. The people in Medjugorje exercise the ecumenical tenet that we are all one in God. It is human-kind who has divided the pie into so many pieces and built walls around our faiths.

The most obvious sign of the presence of Mary is the many unexplained occurrences and miraculous healings that have taken place in the last ten years. Perhaps every one of us wants to see a miracle. But because we live in a world of science and manufactured special effects, we are suspicious of unex-plained occurrences because scientists have so often succeeded in explaining what once was believed to be extraordinary phe-nomena. Why then have Mary's apparition and the resulting unexplained phenomena not been scientifically explained? Scientists from all over the world have studied the children, the villagers, the soil, the atmosphere, and many other seen and unseen scientific manifestations, and they still cannot explain the events.

As with anything that is baffling, there are always more rumors, claims of unusual experiences or events, and exagger-ations than there are substantiated facts. So, without getting bogged down into listing specific miracles, any one of which could be challenged, I will broadly discuss what has taken place over the course of ten years. There have been hundreds of reported healings. I was told by our guide that over eight hundred people have reported being healed of afflictions and that five hundred of the healings have been medically docu-mented. Even if only half of these numbers are correct, it is an incredibly high incidence of unexplained, spontaneous med-ical reversals. Also some of these healings include complete restoration to health from diseases and conditions for which there are no known cures or where doctors have determined that there was no chance for recovery. Doctors have been known to be wrong and miracles occur elsewhere, but in Medjugorje the cures are a part of the ongoing testimony to the faith occurrences.

The children (now adults) are the most visible sign that the apparitions are genuine. As Wayne Weible, who has written many books about Medjugorje, states, "In fact the age and character of all the seers and the consistency of the apparitions with them is strong evidence that something mighty unusual is happening" (1985). These special children have given up their privacy, the years of their youth, and, in some cases, their careers, in order to serve their Holy Mother. They have been probed, wired to instruments, questioned, examined, and stuck with needles to see if they were telling the truth. The question that has to be asked is whether six children would endure all of this for ten years if the apparitions were false. I have climbed both hills, and I can tell you I would not do it again for a lie. Yet these young people climb the hills every few days to experience additional apparitions. Between Mass, rosary, and prayer, they spend a minimum of three hours a day in church. In addition, the villagers have attended rosary, Mass, and healing services for approximately three hours every night for the last ten years. Would they all do this if they doubted the veracity of the visions? Churches in the United States have difficulty getting people to attend Mass for even one hour a week!

Through all of these trials, the visionaries have remained steadfast, calm, and confident. When you speak to them or hear them speak, there is a sense of honesty, integrity, and commitment that is unrivaled.

There are many other miracles or special phenomena that millions of people have experienced while on pilgrimage to Medjugorje. Unfortunately, these can easily become the focus of the experiences instead of ancillary gifts from our Mother. The "miracle of the sun" is seen by some pilgrims, who report being able to look directly into the sun while a disk blocks the hurtful rays. This disk is spoken of as a eucharistic Host. Some see a cross on the disk, others report seeing Mary with baby Jesus in her arms, while still others, watching the sun, report seeing spinning colors, circular rainbows, and colorful rays.

It is hard to estimate how many millions of rosaries have changed from a silver color to a golden color. I personally have seen eight or nine rosaries change, while identical rosaries did not. No one really knows why or how this occurs, though there are many speculations and rumors. When this occurred to my daughters' rosaries, it took my breath away.

There are many other manifestations of a divine presence, some of which are contained in the following chapters, but the greatest miracle is in the hearts of the men, women, and children who spend a week or more in the area. Since we have free will to respond to circumstances as we wish, it is possible for someone to leave after a week and not have experienced any heart conversion, but I observe that this is rare. Almost all people come away with much more than they expected. Some see and experience miracles, others do not. For those who do not behold an actual miracle, the initial disappointment fades and there occurs a deeper miracle. Soon the heart love (my term for the deep feeling of love) grows so strong that it indeed becomes a miracle to the person. If you ask those who have been to Medjugorje to choose between the external manifestations of miracles and the internal miracle, the resounding answer would be to choose the internal one. However, none of us would turn down seeing a miracle.

So why is Mary appearing now, and what are her intentions? We are privy only to some of the answers. Our Mother has told the visionaries that these are dangerous times for the world's inhabitants, that there is a struggle occurring between good and evil, and that there will be strong temptations to heed the world's view of right and wrong and ignore God's. Look around! She is here to teach us, guide us, and point the way.

The visionaries are being given ten secrets that will be unfolding after the apparitions are over (Mary makes it sound as if this will occur in the near future). Mirjana has been chosen by Mary to release each secret at an instructed time to a priest selected by Mirjana. After fasting, the priest will notify the world of the first secret three days before it occurs. As each visionary receives all ten secrets, he or she ceases having daily apparitions and sees Mary only on special occasions or when Mary wishes to address a specific topic. At present, two of the six visionaries have received all ten secrets, and the other four visionaries have received nine secrets.

There have been many speculations about the ten secrets, but very little is known. Some of the events are chastisements for the world, while others are signs (one of which will be an indestructible sign left in Medjugorje) to prove to nonbelievers that the visions are real.

This information is not meant to frighten anyone. It is being given to us so that we do not become frightened or lose faith. The revelation is a blessed gift from the spiritual mother of us all. She wants us to trust God and pray to him and gain strength, so that when the chastisements begin we will remain faithful and not be tempted to leave our Father's protection.

All six of the visionaries say that the secrets, in substance, affect the whole world. There are private secrets for some of them (the seers) concerning their own futures and other secrets relating to the whole world. Only one of the secrets has been revealed by the visionaries. Our Lady has promised to leave a visible sign on the mountain where she first appeared. These are our Lady's words about the sign: "This sign will be given for the atheists. You faithful already have signs and you have to become the sign for the atheists. You faithful must not wait for the sign before you convert: convert soon. This time is a time of grace for you. You can never thank God enough for his grace. The time is for deepening your faith and for your conversion. When the sign comes, it will be too late for many" (Weible 1985).

As of this writing, the world has been to war and ended the war; Yugoslavia is plagued by internal revolution; volcanos have recently erupted; earthquakes have occurred; typhoons have struck; our streets are filled with crime and drugs; and the headline story each evening is about Jeffrey Dahmer's killing, mutilating, and cannibalizing more than a dozen young people. What the world needs now is exactly what our Mother is calling us all to—love, peace, conversion to God, and prayer.

As you read the following chapters, notice the themes that seem to surface over and over again through each author's account of Medjugorje: the lack of understanding in feeling the call to go to Medjugorje, and the subsequent yielding to that call; the feelings of peace and love that pervade each experience; the giving over or giving up of some trait or thing that was felt to be important; the acceptance of all people, creeds, and religions; feeling welcomed, accepted, and included in the events of Medjugorje; the wish to experience "miracles," coming to accept this need to "see something" as a normal curiosity and the eventual ability to experience miracles as adjunctive to the trip, not the main focus; the experiencing of God's love and the internal manifestation of that love as the real miracle; the desire to share experiences without pushing ideas onto others; God's gift of Mary as one of the most precious gifts of all; the almost apologetic tone of each account; the firm conviction that Mary is indeed appearing to the visionaries; the change of their hearts without a change in who they are as people; the understanding and acceptance of the fact that their experiences do not "fix" everything in their lives but bring a peace during the trials of life; a blending of the beauty of their particular religious perspective with their experience of Medjugorje and Roman Catholicism.

Some have chosen to make Catholicism their religious avenue, while others remain firm in their belief that they are worshipping in the faith community that best represents who they are. The joy of this book is that the authors are all ordinary people who have been touched deeply. No one is a professional theologian or writer or claims to have all the answers. What they do share are their own special experiences, which have strong commonalities: their love for God, the unfolding of the importance of Mary's appearance, and their belief and acceptance of their catholic (universal) experience as the true way that God wants us to relate to each other.

*D*ear children, during these days people
from all nations will be coming into the
parish. And now I am calling you to love:
love first of all your own household members,
and then you will be able to accept and love
all who are coming. Thank you for having
responded to my call.

—Message given to visionaries by Mary,
June 6, 1985

A Lutheran's Perspective
of Medjugorje

Sharon E. Cheston

T he following is a letter I wrote on December 19, 1989, the night before I left for Medjugorje.

Most Holy Father, Lord Jesus, Holy Spirit and Blessed Mother,

I must confide that I have always believed that you personally care and love me and all people of the world. As a child I had the faith of a child. As an adolescent, I was strongly drawn to the church through several mentors you sent to care for me spiritually. Although I have made many mistakes in my life, not the least of which was my relationship with my parents, my betrayal of a friend, a professional mistake in judgment and many many times when I placed earthly pleasure above my love for you; I have not doubted your existence or plan for my life.

If I have any regrets, I regret that I have not spent the whole of my 42+ years totally dedicating myself to you. I have worked more than I prayed, gossiped more than I worked, busied myself more than I centered myself, and questioned more than accepted.

At middle age I am overwhelmed by your generosity of your call. First, I am not worthy. I know that everyone says that but I am not! I have not the theological background, nor the speaking strength nor the writing ability to witness as is befitting such a miraculous God. There are others much more skilled and much more deserving. But here I am with a miracle on my hands and I am about to burst. I have so many questions that I know You cannot answer . . . not now, maybe someday.

In August, 1988, I read a newspaper article by Wayne Weible on the miracle of Medjugorje. As I read, I knew that the apparitions were true, not in my head but in my heart. One month later my neighbor announced that she was going to Medjugorje with her family. At the time I remember feeling very thrilled that she was going and taking our family's crosses with her. I also felt drawn to go but was put off by the poor conditions and the lack of amenities. Joy said that if I was meant to go it would happen. Joy's friend said that Mary had reached out and touched my heart and that not everyone has to go. "Blessed are they that do not see but still believe." Somehow I was comforted by that. I did not have to go to Medjugorje to be blessed. But over the next year, I prayed more and more, I read more, I let go of control and the more I did all of the above, the more I felt called to go to Medjugorje. By summer of '89 I had a dilemma. I wanted to go (sorta), but I could not justify going without my family who also spoke of going, and I could not afford for all of us to go given having two in college at the same time in 1990.

Then in August of '89 while on vacation I read Wayne Weible's book *Medjugorje: The Message*. I sat at Cedar Knob Resort on the beach in a bathing suit and cried tears of joy. I shared the book with my teenage girls and they were touched too. In October I decided to verbalize what I had been kicking around for a month and was afraid to say. I asked my husband if he were willing to give up exchanging Christmas presents and spend the money on a trip to Medjugorje. Jim said, "Sure!" I was stunned. I asked if he thought that the girls would do the same. He said, "I think that you'll be surprised." I called my college child. Her reaction was, "Mom, I'm surprised that you had to ask . . . of course." My senior in high school said, "Make the reservations." I was speechless. Teenagers giving up Christmas gifts seemed like a miracle to me.

Of course, I was assuming that there would be a tour going. In some way I knew that we were going. I just did not know how. I called Caritas in Birmingham, but they had no trips at Christmas and they really discouraged me. Then I remembered reading in Wayne's book about another message center in the northeast. I flipped through the book and the words jumped out at me: "Center for Peace in Boston." I called information and got the number.

John Murphy was on duty at the time of my call and I told my story.

1) My family was willing to give up their gifts to get a more blessed gift.

2) I had teens who could not get away easily because of school and jobs so Christmastime was the perfect time.

3) This is the year of Family Unity and this fact is empowering us. John said that he was touched and would get back to me.

When I got off the phone I prayed. I said, "Dear Lord, I have tried to find a tour with little success. If you want us to go, please help me find a way. As you know, I am into control, but I give this over to your hands. God and Blessed Mother, do as You will." At that moment, I felt that all would work out, but I did not know why.

Three weeks later, John called to say that the Center had put together a pilgrimage on December 26 through January 2 and it was to be called "The Christmas Gift Pilgrimage." My heart and mind were racing. I cried, I said that I knew I would be going, and I thanked God. Then I felt fear, but I trusted. I took my Christmas savings ($1,800) and sent the deposit. I still owed $3,600 and was unsure how to make this money appear. I worked the budget in my head and arrived at a plan. I was going to create a loan and pay it off over the next 3–4 months. I wrote the final check and mailed it, uttering a small prayer about God letting me be able to pay it off over the next 3–4 months. Three days later a check arrived from the American Red Cross for $3,200. It appears that they closed out all of the small investments in the Retirement Fund. I never contributed to the Fund and believed that I was not vested because I only served for 4 years, not the 5 that was required. When I opened the check I burst into tears and fell to my knees. I have never experienced anything so powerful in all my life. Some may say that this is all coincidence. I have felt coincidence and I have felt God, and this was God's work. You know the feeling of shivering inside when you look upon your sleeping infant and see the beauty and love of the world wrapped up in the several pounds of love? Well, this feeling was like every one of those moments happening all at once. It was a physical upheaval. I shook, laughed, cried, yielded, and questioned. Why me? I don't know. I am no one particularly special. I'm an above-average teacher with above-average intelligence living in a wonderful family with a little too much income so that I've become a little too complacent. I work hard, but I'm spiritually lazy. Perhaps it is not me at all who is being called; perhaps it is my children or spouse. Perhaps I am simply the catalyst. This makes sense to me, since I think that my family members are much better at expressing their ideas than I.

However, I do have one gift that maybe God can use. People trust me and trust my judgment. When I talk about my experiences and views, others give credence to what I say. But I have so much inside and I cannot sort it all out, let alone tell others so they'll understand. Dear God, why didn't You call Scott Peck or Bob Wicks to Medjugorje? They can write and speak so eloquently. I bet they don't have to use a thesaurus to sound good or a dictionary to look up how to spell thesaurus! I guess the "Why me" is not important. God, Your will is hard to comprehend. (Notice I used "comprehend" and not "understand." That is because my thesaurus works!)

I am afraid, Lord, that I will let You down, that I will disappoint others because I cannot find the words, that I will lose friends because of my experience or that I will become too full of self instead of full of You. I like to be liked and accepted. Already I have felt the silence from some friends and family when I offer my ideas concerning Medjugorje. The strange thing is that although I do feel the sting of rejection, my deeper concern is for their seeming rejection of You. I grow sad and feel lost to them. How much worse You must feel, for You created them.

So here I sit one week from the day of departure. I have many mixed feelings, but I have trust in Your wisdom, and I have faith that You will show me what You want me to do and how. Lord, I only hope that I am up to the challenge.

The above letter was written on the eve of a trip that would change my life. As I sit and write this chapter, I am still the same person, in the same house, at the same job, but there is something deep inside that has shifted. As I go to speak to groups of my experience, I share that prior to Medjugorje I had all the . . . right stuff . . . of a faithful person. I attended church regularly, I had been baptized and confirmed, I attempted to be good (and failed), I prayed, and I read the Bible. But when I made the pilgrimage, it was as if God took all those ingredients and did something special with them. It was like milk, eggs, butter, flour, and so on, being transformed into a cake. Well, I guess God baked a cake inside of me. Actually, one of the blessings I received was the realization that God is still baking the cake and will continue to improve on the project until I reach perfection, which will be long after I have left this world. This book is a part of my baking. It has been a gift and a challenge. But above all, I pray that whoever reads these chapters will be touched in some way so that God enriches the soul. If, as you read, you feel something resonating inside of you, I would ask that you consider that Mary, your mother, is calling to you. She loves everyone and is calling each of us to come back to God. Every faith journey is important no matter what religion you have chosen wherein to demonstrate your faith. Your journey, your perspective is precious and important. While others and I share our journeys with you, you have your own. Mary asks us to live our faith, and she is here, during a difficult world situation, to help us by giving us messages and information that will aid our souls' growth and development. I know of people who have daily rituals that are designed to improve and maintain their physical health through diet and exercise. I know of people who daily improve themselves intellectually by continuing to read, take courses, or study. I know of people who monitor emotions and work every day to clarify their myriad feelings. Why is it that our greatest and most precious component, our spiritual self, is left for one day a week or only one hour a week? The physical, emotional, and intellectual components will die, but our souls live on. Each day we should exercise, caress, challenge, and move our souls to a better place, just as we exercise our bodies or challenge ourselves intellectually.

This was always my philosophy but never my practice. At best it was haphazard and half-baked. Medjugorje changed all that for me. Here is my story. I pray that it is as accurate and honest a presentation as I can give, and I ask God to guide my pen.

As my family and I approached the airport, I felt fear and excitement. My husband, Jim, was already taking his managerial role seriously by organizing and directing our movements. My two daughters, Shannon, age 20, and Kelly, age 17, were apprehensive but looked sure of themselves. The plane was very crowded, and we were forced to separate, but after many seat adjustments I somehow ended up sitting next to Sister Jane Culligan, our group's spiritual director. Jane and I began talking, and I related my story of how I had come to this point. About an hour outside New York the plane began to experience turbulence. This was worse than most I had experienced while traveling. Jane asked if I wanted to say the rosary and I was startled. I never had said the rosary out loud with another person, and I, as a Lutheran, was just learning it. But considering the turbulence, I felt that it would not hurt, so we began. The turbulence continued throughout the entire five decades. At the end, Jane said a prayer asking for a smooth flight, and immediately the plane ride calmed as the turbulence ceased. I was impressed and grateful. Jane and I then began talking about what we were experiencing, and I mentioned that the turbulence seemed like a struggle over the plane, almost as if a person was on each wing tugging. No sooner were these words out of my mouth when the turbulence returned, but this time it was much worse. People were becoming ill, the stewards and stewardesses were yelling at people to stay in their seats, the ceiling grommets were pulling apart, and water was dripping into the plane. Jane picked up her rosary and I quickly followed with no reservations. After saying a decade I felt weak and faint, and Jane, never missing a Hail Mary, took out Holy Oil and anointed me. As a Lutheran I had never experienced this before and was even unsure as to what she was doing. However, as she blessed me, my fear left me, and I began to feel well enough to continue the rosary. Jane then took out Holy Water and began sprinkling the plane, asking for whatever was causing the plane's turbulence to leave, and then she prayed for a smooth and safe trip. Immediately, the plane's ride calmed and we did not experience another bump or rattle.

I had to look at my concept of coincidence, and throughout the rest of the week I had to look at this again and again until I realized coming home that I did not believe in coincidence any longer. This was a major shift in me. My doctoral dissertation taught me about randomness and chance events. Here, I was saying that chance does not exist. Was I stepping off into the deep end of a pool where I could drown? Would my colleagues back home think that I was crazy? I did not care.

Medjugorje is a beautiful little town, with the church dominating the scene and a mountainous view that takes your breath away. We stayed with a local family who did not speak English, but somehow we managed to communicate, and our interpreter, Marina, was of great help.

The first day began with a trip to see Ivan (pronounced E–van), one of the visionaries. His mission is to reach out to youth and their families. On our way there, Jim was organizing and directing us as if he had been there all his life. Jane commented on this and asked Jim if he were a manager on his job. Eventually Jim replied yes and Jane said, "Good, we could use a manager." I felt compelled to add that Jim manages everything and that we call him MOW—Manager of the World.

Ivan talked for what seemed like thirty to forty minutes, and as a psychotherapist I was struck with how easily this simple peasant man was speaking of family systems theory as well as other complex psychological constructs. However, Ivan was not using "psychobabble." He was speaking directly and concretely. He paused and then said, "Fathers should stop trying to be managers in their families and begin joining their families as members." The statement may have been lost on most listeners, but it was not lost on the Chestons. We were all stunned, amazed, and baffled. Coincidence was challenged again. After Ivan's talk, our group climbed the Hill of Apparitions. No one prepared me for this. The hill is rocky, steep, and slippery. I ran out of breath and kept looking for the top. Twice my foot slipped and my ankle turned so that my ankle bone hit the ground. I was positive that I would have sprained or bruised it, but I did not hurt it at all. No bruise ever appeared. Puzzling, grappling thoughts haunted me.

The top of the hill was so peaceful. Each person respected the space of others. Some were praying, others were saying the rosary, and others were singing. I just stood there and tried to imagine Mary appearing to some frightened teenagers.

The next night we climbed the hill again because Mary was to appear at 10:30 P.M. This time our ascent was in the dark. All those rocks and steep paths were now only visible with the help of a flashlight on them. I remember looking up the hill and wondering how I was going to possibly reach the top and cursing all the food that I had eaten that made me feel too heavy to make the climb. I put my head down and prayed "Mary help me" and began in my head singing "Ave Maria." I was only mildly aware of the strain of climbing, and I remember looking for the halfway mark and not seeing it. Then I heard Jim say, "We're here," and I looked up to see the most jet black sky I had ever seen with the brightest stars. I was astonished. "I made it!"

The cross that marks the top was lit from below with many candles, and it was easy to focus on it. Since it was January, the weather was cool and the climb made me hot. But then as I cooled down I began to shiver. At 10:30 P.M. someone whom I could not see said to kneel and face the cross because the vision had begun. I was miserable, I was cold, my knees were on rocks, my back hurt, and I could not remember what I had come eight thousand miles to say in prayer. I began to cry and I could not or would not stop. I remember at one point asking Mary to wrap her mantle around me to make me warm, and I instantly felt warm. Then I remember questioning why this had happened, and I was instantly cold. I was probably the most pitiful, miserable person on the mountain. With Jesus' mother appearing no more than fifty feet away I could do nothing but cry. When I arrived back at the house I realized that I was very sick; I had a significant fever and my chest seemed full. I could not understand it. When we left the house at 9:15 I was fine, but at midnight I was so sick I could barely talk without my chest hurting.

The next day was highlighted with a trip to see Vicka (pronounced Vis–ka), another visionary. During the mile walk between villages, my daughter Shannon began talking about the trip. She stated that she was angry and disappointed. She had felt nothing on the mountain the previous night. She said that she had been frightened and sickened by the plane ride, that she had been doing everything that Mary had asked (like saying the rosary), and that she had felt nothing on the mountain. Others had seen the sun dance and had their rosaries turn a golden color, but nothing had happened to her. I was feeling so miserable with my chest and fever that I could not talk and walk at the same time. But Jim jumped in and told a story (parable?) about when he was a little boy and wanted to earn an award at camp. He tried and tried. He did everything to win the award, but it went to someone else. After the award's ceremony Jim asked the camp counselor why he had not been given the award, and the counselor replied that he *had tried too hard*. Likewise, his advice to Shannon was to be herself and to stop trying to be perfect, because God loves us just the way we are.

Vicka was glowing, radiant, and beautiful. At the end of our time with her she was answering questions in Croatian while an interpreter translated. At one moment she looked at Shannon and said, "Be done with trivial things. Stop worrying about rosaries turning gold or seeing the sun dance. You are here because God has called you here. He loves you." Shannon looked stunned and then began to cry. Through the tears she said that Vicka must have been walking behind us listening to our conversation. I smiled and replied, "Shannon, Vicka does not speak English." That night Shannon prayed a different prayer. She prayed that she could let go of the trivial manifestations of Mary's presence. But being the human being that she is, she also prayed for a tiny little sign. The next day on her way to rosary, Shannon saw the sun dance. Jim was with her and attests to the fact that there were no clouds in the sky. The sun was so bright that he could not look at it, but Shannon was looking directly into the sun for approximately fifteen minutes as they walked. A small (but significant) sign, just as she had requested.

On one of the following days, our group climbed Mount Krizevac, but I was unable to do this due to my fever and congestion. I must say I was relieved, because I had been told that it was a brutal, difficult climb that could take two hours. When my family returned they were exhilarated and exhausted, but they all concurred that the climb was much harder than the climb up the Hill of Apparitions. This mountain stood as a challenge and a threat to me. I was sure I could not ever climb it. A year later I was proven wrong.

One of the most powerful events of any trip to Medjugorje is visiting with Father Jozo, who was the priest of Saint James parish when the apparitions began. When we made our trip in 1989, Father Jozo (pronounced Yo–zo) was serving a parish forty-five minutes away from Medjugorje. Because we had heard that he truly is a saint on earth, we traveled to Father Jozo's parish to hear him speak. He told us that at first he had doubted the authenticity of the apparitions when they began. But after he personally saw Mary in the church during a mass (in fact the whole worshiping body saw and heard her), he became the children's protector. He even served one and a half years in prison for refusing to curtail the apparitions (Weible, 1989). He radiates his joy, commitment, and faith. His power is startling. We sat for almost three hours listening, praying, and singing, and it felt like thirty minutes. On the way back to Medjugorje, the group decided to say the rosary, and as people began to pull their rosaries out of pockets and knapsacks, I could hear gasps as several discovered that their silver rosaries had turned to a beautiful bright gold color. Holding those rosaries filled me with wonder and gave me a sense of how little we know about God's world and power.

The most miraculous part of Medjugorje has little to do with transforming rosaries or ocular abnormalities that permit one to look directly into the sun without hurting one's eyes. My rosary did not turn colors and I did not see the miracle of the sun on that trip, but something else did occur that I am only recently beginning to appreciate.

I now have trouble receiving Communion without crying, I have the ability to pray in a manner that seems less routine and more sincere, I am more able to let others be who they are, and I feel a sense of peace even when horrendous things around and within me are happening. Of course I fail at all of the above as often as I succeed, but there is a difference that I can feel.

Returning from Medjugorje was like going from ten miles an hour to warp speed. My life seemed to have suspended itself for a week while I was there, but upon returning I could feel all the pressures of life emerge once again. I would love to tell you that since returning my life has been perfect. It has not. In fact, I have experienced the most challenging, agonizing, and growth-producing months of my life. I returned naively thinking that if I tried to be perfect and humble, I would be protected by God from life's pains. My immature faith view was certainly challenged in the two years that followed. Everything that I held dear in this world was either taken from me or was seriously threatened to be taken away. I experienced death of a loved one, accidents, illness, discord, and natural catastrophes. I had to completely rethink the meaning of this life on earth and what really is important. Every step on this journey Christ has been there with encouragement. Mary has soothed my pain and brushed away my tears. To feel their presence even though I did not understand the reasons behind the events still brought peace.

Throughout all these trials I have struggled and struggled with the "Why?" and have come to no answer. I feel as if I am on a personal journey that in some way is important, but I am in no way privy to the reasons behind the pain. The most amazing part is that the strength of Medjugorje has stayed with me. I found a loving Mother there who is continually pointing the way to her Son who leads me directly to my God. As a Lutheran, I was always taught that Mary was a sweet, pure Jewish girl whom God chose to bear his Son to the world. I never saw her as my mother, only as Jesus' Mother. I know now that she is so much more, and I feel cheated out of knowing her during the earlier part of my life. I remember being critical of Roman Catholics who worshipped Mary and was frankly skeptical when I heard that some Yugoslavian children were seeing her daily and had been given messages for the world. I expected to hear Roman Catholic dogma to be continuously pronounced at Mass. But I did not hear what I expected. This is probably why I was able to consider the visions as being real. The messages were for *me* and they are as embraceable for a Lutheran as they are for any other religion. Mary proposes five areas for us to consider.

Commitment to God

Mary encourages all of us to let God rule our lives. To do this we must place God before all other earthly wants and turn away from anything that would cause us to be alienated from God. Every minute of your life belongs to God. We tend to narcissistically call our lives our own. We did not create our lives, so they are not ours. The only way we can claim these lives as ours is if we walk away from God.

Faith

Mary calls faith our lifeline to God. But having faith and living our faith are very different. We are called to a life in faith.

Peace

Who does not wish for peace? But to obtain peace we need to have peace within us, and then we can begin having peace in our human relationships, and through these we can have peace in our war-threatened world.

Prayer

Mary asks that we do not pray to her but to pray as if she is standing beside us helping us to pray. Does she intercede for me? I sure hope so. I do not believe that I need to have someone intercede for me with Christ or God, because I believe in a personal God to whom I can readily speak directly, honestly, and openly. But I am glad to have Mary's help in any way she sees fit to assist me as my spiritual mother.

Mary also revealed to the children that she is the mother of all of us, not just Roman Catholics. She is calling all of us back to God, and she is asking for a conversion, not to Roman Catholicism, but to the heart of God.

Mary encourages us to pray, to pray with the heart and to pray every day as much as humanly possible. She specifically asks us to pray for peace. In addition, she wants us to attend our churches' services. In Medjugorje they attend church for three hours every day, and the church is packed.

Fasting

Fasting was difficult for me, not because it was Catholic but because I am not used to it and it seemed meaningless. Mary asks those of us who can to fast on bread and water two times per week, Wednesdays and Fridays. At first I was taken aback. Why Wednesdays and Fridays? Why not Tuesdays? Why two times and not three or one? Could coffee or tea be substituted for water? I tried it and I didn't like it. I felt nauseous. Then I heard the purpose behind fasting from Father Jozo, and it began to make more sense. As I prayed, I was able to let go of all the rules and regulations and focus on the purpose. Also, Mary has related to the children that people who do not wish to fast from food may fast from other things like alcohol, cigarettes, sweets, or even a negative behavior like losing one's temper. The important aspect is to give up a negative behavior that one seems to enjoy. By doing this we gain control over the negative behavior; we offer the behavior to God as our way of trying to be a better person and we strengthen our selves. It is a sacrifice, albeit a small one, but it emulates the tradition of sacrifice of our forefathers and foremothers. Also, by fasting we emulate Jesus' sacrifice. Life is full of sacrifices, and by consciously offering up a sacrifice we gain more than we give up. Once again I ask you to pray about this topic. You may be surprised at the answer that you will receive.

My second trip to Medjugorje, in January of 1991, was as the leader of a thirty-three-person group. The call to go again was strong, but I did not want to go. The first trip had been rough and I had been sick most of the time. In addition, I needed to put into practice the teachings I had heard, and I did not have enough time to do that before I returned. However, my timetable and God's were incompatible, so I let go of mine. Leading a group was not my idea either, but once you turn your life over to God you lovingly accept the challenges ahead of you.

As I walked to church my first morning I could see Mount Krizevac above the church and felt called to climb it. Despite the fact that I had spent the year working out and losing some weight, I was still not confident that my genetically poor knees would sustain me on the climb. But I had several days to consider it, so I put it off and was grateful to do so.

The group was an amazing conglomeration of talents, needs, beliefs, and experiences. They jelled and loved immediately. They began to experience what I had experienced—one coincidence on top of another that soon becomes no coincidence. Each person had a story to tell about the trip, and each one received much more than expected. Each would have to tell his or her story because I could never do it justice. I can only tell you mine. On this trip I did see the miracle of the sun and watched it on two different occasions for ten to fifteen minutes each. The first time was with a group who had taken a side trip to Mostar. Seven or eight people in our bus saw the sun and were watching. Two of us tried to look and couldn't. I then decided to pray. I told God that I was very angry because I did not want to need to see a miracle, but I knew that I was too weak and I did need to see, especially if everyone else was experiencing it. I opened my eyes and saw the miracle of the sun. I was able to look directly at the sun for fifteen minutes with no physical discomfort or lasting effects.

I also climbed Mount Krizevac! I chose Friday, a day I would fast, and I prayed to be alone as I climbed. When I started up the mountain I inadvertently took a wrong path and only saw two people during the climb. The climb was not nearly as rocky and difficult as I had been led to believe, but it was a physically exhausting experience. When I reached the top I realized that I had discovered the "back door" path, but my needs had been met. I was alone and I was able to climb. From the top you feel you can see forever. The many-ton cross is extraordinary. Just thinking of the townspeople carrying all the cement and water on their backs to the top to build it in 1933 left me in awe of the faith and courage it took. And here I was worried about just being able to walk up the path! On the way back I decided to climb down the front path. It was unbelievable. The rocks, really boulders, were waist high, and I was constantly hyperextending my knees to get over them. It started to rain, and the rocks became slippery while the path turned to mud. It was a difficult, fear-filled, and dangerous climb down. Once I reached the bottom, I realized that had I discovered the frontal approach going up, I would have probably given up and not tried the ascent. God gives us exactly what we can handle.

Through these years of troubles the experience on Mount Krizevac stood as a symbol for persevering through the difficult, fear-filled, and dangerous times. It was not until I was preparing to leave Medjugorje the second time that I remembered another dangerous, fearful experience I had had. When I was a small child I had rheumatic fever and my pastor brought me a five-inch plain white cross that stood on two steps. It was made out of a material that glowed in the dark. As I stood on the step of the bus to leave Medjugorje, I recognized Mount Krizevac as an almost exact duplication of my little plastic cross. Why had I never seen this "coincidence" before? And, in addition, many people have witnessed Mount Krizevac glowing at night on the mountain. As I rode the bus to the airport I was silent, overwhelmed by this parting gift. I wondered what had happened to my little cross. I could not wait to get home and look for it. The first memorabilia box I opened contained the treasured cross.

May God's blessing always be upon you.

J *oy will manifest in your hearts and thus*
you shall be joyful witnesses of that which
my Son and I want from each of you.

—Message given to visionaries by Mary,
February 25, 1987

A Presbyterian Lay Person's Perspective of Medjugorje

Joy Lemmon

I did not know why I wanted to go to Medjugorje. Ours was a dual-religion marriage; my husband practiced Catholicism and I attended the Presbyterian church. The children had been christened Catholic, but shortly thereafter it was decided that it would be best for all if I would oversee the religious training. So, on Sunday mornings my husband went to Mass, and the children and I went to Sunday school and church. As the children grew older, it became a ritual each Sunday to meet after church at a restaurant for a "special" breakfast, and the conversation always turned to comparing sermons. This was a special time for our family, and the ecumenical spirit was an integral part of our family life.

When my close friend, Anne, arrived home from her trip to Medjugorje, she brought each member of my family a rosary and a medal. My husband Lowell and I listened to her glowing account of her experiences, and, I guess, it was then the desire to go was ignited. Several months later, when we were watching a program on television about Medjugorje, Lowell looked at me and said, "Would you like to go?" I wanted to go, but I also wanted to take our adult children. My daughter Kim was then 30, married, and had a six-month-old baby girl, Kalyn. Her husband, Craig, was employed in North Carolina where they had only recently relocated. It was highly unlikely that he would be able to take an extended week off from work. My son, Lowell, Jr., then 27, was in similar circumstances in the Baltimore area.

By the time we heard of the next scheduled pilgrimage, there was very little time to try to arrange everything . . . passports, visas, and so on. The manner in which the trip all came together and everyone was freed up to go was a miracle. The

entire trip preparation was so facile that it was still unbelievable to me as we were enplaning for Medjugorje in September
1988—jobs still intact, baby happily ensconced with trusted
family members, and carrying rosaries and religious articles
entrusted to our care for blessings. During the preparation
for the trip, I had a small portrait pin of our baby Kalyn made
as a surprise for Kim. I gave it to her saying, "Kalyn can go
with us over your heart." Kim never took it off—so we felt
complete as a family.

After a grueling twenty-four-hour journey, we reached our
destination in the town of Medjugorje just before the Croatian
evening Mass at Saint James Church. We dropped our belong-
ings and headed for the church on foot. Here I witnessed and
participated in the most beautiful Mass I ever saw. I was in awe
of the people . . . their faces . . . their prayerfulness . . . the
beautiful resounding response of the rosary . . . the peace!
This little church was jammed with pilgrims from all over the
world, leaving very little room for the local peasants to worship, and yet I found them gracious as they would crowd
together on the pews to accommodate us. Words are difficult
to come by, but there was a holiness about the service. I shall
never forget that first night, singing the "Battle Hymn of the
Republic," holding hands with my husband, and truly feeling
the presence of our Lady. The Mass was concelebrated by
thirty or forty priests from many different countries. People
were standing in the aisles, sitting on the floor, and even man-
aging to squeeze onto the kneeler edges for a seat. The
church was so overly filled that the crowd spilled out into the
surrounding countryside, even into the vineyards, where
priests of different orders were hearing confession. So holy!
The evening ended with dinner in a little Croatian home and
a short discussion by our whole group of our first impressions.
Our beds were welcome sights!

The first day was the celebration of the fifty-fifth anniversary of the erection of the cross on Mount Krizevac. Festival
Day! The cross had been erected on the mountain in 1933 to
commemorate the nineteen hundredth anniversary of Christ's
crucifixion. Different clans came from all over Yugoslavia to
participate. That day all who were able to make the trip climbed
to the top of the mountain to celebrate the Mass. We arose,

ate hurriedly, dressed, grabbed our already loaded backpacks, and, as a group, joined the throngs of people headed in the direction of Mount Krizevac. The walk on the dusty country lane became a village road crowded with people and cars. The day was hot and the excitement of festival was everywhere. The crowd swallowed us up, and soon we were being hustled and shoved along. The road abruptly turned left and became a steep rocky path. The climb became progressively harder, steeper, and rockier. The local villagers, peasants, and tourists (mostly foreign but basically European) were jostling us onward and upward. Some were praying the rosary as they walked, other groups were singing, some were entire families meeting for the festival, many were barefooted. Along the way, we stopped to rest where we could find the footing to balance ourselves. As we progressed up the mountain we noticed the fourteen Stations of the Cross were marked by large, beautiful bronze plaques erected in special locations among the rocks. At each station we stopped to read from our prayer book— first Lowell, then me, then Kim, then her husband, Craig, and finally Lowell, Jr. We continued to take turns. The prayers we read were like talking to the Blessed Mother about each sorrow she endured on her Son's path to Calvary. There was Scripture, a prayer for forgiveness, and finally there were our Lady's own words as represented by the visionaries of Medjugorje. Even though we randomly took turns reading, the prayers seemed custom made for each member, as they touched us deeply.

We cried as a family, we consoled, and we laughed. It was like a confession for all of us. It was the most touching experience I have ever participated in and witnessed. My family was never so close. I felt the presence of our Lord, and I thanked him for this privilege. The higher we climbed, the greater became the physical challenge. The people amazed me because everyone began helping each other. If you slipped, someone caught you, and even though your "thank you" was not understood, your rescuer simply patted your hand and smiled. You, in turn, did the same, and your heart grew bigger and bigger. I loved the faces, the weathered smiles, the poverty of the people who sang and ate their fruit and insisted on sharing.

One man came over to me and put his bottle of schnapps to my mouth and insisted I drink. I drank! Then he dumped his grapes into Craig's backpack. His generosity so over-whelmed us that we reciprocated with some of our dried banana flakes.

When we reached the top, where the Mass was just begin-ning, there was no room to stand or sit. Because there were thousands of people crowded onto the mountaintop, we were balancing at times on just one foot. My greatest joy involved a tiny peasant lady who nudged me aside, squirmed her way down to the ground, and sat on my foot. This totally robbed me of any footing I had, so Lowell, Jr., and I clung to each other for support. When he finally managed to find a spot and sat down on the ground, I lost my footing completely and landed on his lap. This caused much laughter and smiles from those around us, and from that point on we seemed to be included in their group.

When Mass was almost over, the same peasant lady who had "stolen" my footing got up to take Communion and struggled to get her sandals on. The whole scene was so funny . . . I can still picture her shy smile and giggle as she tried to balance and stretch her sandals onto her swollen feet. As she bent over, her face was even with mine. I reached up my hand and steadied her arm, and she said, "folla." When she straightened up, she turned and opened her plastic bag filled with tiny apples and offered me one. When she insisted that I take it, rather than offend, I took one and bit into it. It was so deli-cious I guess because of the simple beauty of the giver.

The rest of the day was filled with people singing and danc-ing. A man played a pigskin instrument, and the crowd prayed and picnicked the rest of the day. Happy and exhausted we started the long climb down, which was even more treacher-ous than the hard climb up. There were an estimated one hundred thousand people on Mount Krizevac that day.

The next day we went to the English-speaking Mass. The main celebrant was an Irish priest, and his group comprised the lectors and petition presenters who selected the hymns for the service. The Irish hymn "Gentle Woman" was being sung. Men had their hands and arms raised to heaven singing. My husband and I found tears streaming down our faces. It is absolutely a beautiful hymn, and you could feel the Holy Spirit present. After Mass our group met to walk to Vicka's house. When we arrived, people were crowding into her grape-laden patio. A sister started the rosary, and everyone prayed while we waited. Finally Vicka appeared—radiant and sweet. She told us what "our Lady" wants of us—prayer, fasting, conversion, and peace. She was very patient and generous with her time. I managed with Lowell, Jr.'s, help to have Vicka sign all of our prayer books. We were thrilled.

Our evenings were spent at Masses and prayers. One thing I found extraordinary was that each evening at Saint James, while the rosary was being chanted, the birds would begin to flock into the trees nearest the church and begin their singing. From around six in the evening on, their singing would get louder and louder as the time neared for the apparition. They would be the most boisterous at 6:40, at the time our Lady appeared, and then miraculously they would quiet down and leave. I noticed that this happened each night, and others in our group observed it too.

Each group in Medjugorje has a spiritual director and ours was Father Isaac. Since my son, Lowell, was single, he and Father Isaac shared a room. On the first night, Father invited Lowell to pray with him. Lowell said, "Father, I don't know how to say the rosary, but I will if you teach me." Father taught Lowell, and so each evening Lowell would meet Father in their room at eleven o'clock (Father's bedtime) to join him in the rosary. On one of the evenings, Lowell had gone to the store to get a coke for one of our group members who had become sick. While hurrying down the dark road, he saw three bright flashes of light in the sky. The lights resembled pinpoints of light which then quickly extended horizontally in the sky. He knew it was almost eleven because he was hurrying to meet Father. Lowell, Jr., made a mental note of the location where he was standing in relation to the guest house. Lowell knows that the light was not lightning because it was not crooked or haphazard. He also knows that they were not camera flashes, because he had seen these before and the lights did not resemble the camera flashes he had seen. The next morning he went to see an Irish youth group with whom he had become friendly. They pinpointed the area as being

Apparition Hill. They also told him the visionaries had come up that night and our Lady had appeared with three angels. When Lowell, Jr., asked about what time it had been, they all agreed that it was just before eleven. Then he shared with them what he had seen from his vantage point. They said, "When the angels come, Lowell, they come in light; our Lady simply appears. Don't question it, Lowell, just accept it as a gift from our Lady."

Arrangements had been made for us to go to hear Father Jozo in Tihaljina, about thirty miles from Medjugorje. We boarded the buses along with another group and the rosary was begun. Most joined in while others napped. Finally it grew quiet, and we all became lost in our own thoughts. I had to admire the beautiful scenery—vineyards, enormous mountain ranges, and charming little Spanish tiled villas. I had a long talk with Father Isaac about Catholicism. He is a sweet man and he wanted to help us all.

When we arrived at the church, we entered to find very few seats left. My husband, Lowell, and I were separated since he was taping with video. A hush fell over the church, and I looked up to see a friar enter from the left of the altar. He had a strong face that had a holiness about it, with very soft gentle eyes. He began to speak and I could feel the forcefulness of his words. His voice was melodious and yet strong. Indescribable! I hope that I shall always remember the feeling of being there, and thankfully I have the video Lowell took that day. At times, his message became difficult to understand because interpreters were changed three times trying to keep up with the translation. He explained that people who come to Medjugorje have been called to help witness but that we should not be afraid. He retold the story of the visionaries and ended with our Lady's prayer for conversion, Prayer (with our hearts), Penance, and Fasting.

While listening, a tiny Filipino lady was seated on my right fanning herself. She moved closer, then closer, and finally she fanned me too. I smiled and touched her hand in thanks. I was enchanted with her charity in fanning me too. She reminded me of an eager little child who took such pleasure gaining my approval. After the speech we said goodbye and hugged. Where else would you so easily hug a stranger?

After we had reentered the bus, one person in our group came running back to the bus saying Father Jozo was blessing people (he also has the gift of healing). I jumped up and called to Kim to follow quickly. My two men were outside and we all rushed back into the church. There, at the altar, were small groups of people waiting patiently as Father Jozo moved slowly among them, placing his hands on their heads, saying a prayer, and finishing with the sign of the cross. I had never seen this before, but following the example of others, Kim and I walked forward and waited until it was our turn. Father Jozo turned and put his hand on my head and Kim's simultaneously and began to pray. I heard my husband say, "Father, her jaw" (I have suffered TMJ muscle spasms of the jaw for several years). I don't think Father Jozo understood, for he hesitated. Lowell then placed Father Jozo's hand on my face. This was the strangest feeling. He touched my jaw and pressed in deeply. He prayed and I felt a complete sense of peace. He ended with the sign of the cross on my forehead and Kim's. I had seen another lady hold up her rosary, so I kept my eyes closed and held up all of the medals, crosses, and the rosary I was carrying. He pressed his hand over mine enclosing all of my holy items. I felt the presence of the Holy Spirit. I wanted to cry and smile at the same time, and still I felt unworthy to even be standing there. The funny thing is that I never realized until writing this that my jaw problem cleared up and never returned.

Kim and I walked out arm in arm. At the door we both wept at the wonder of it all. She said through her tears that Father Jozo had looked down at Kalyn's picture and blessed her too. This was the highlight of my trip to Medjugorje. Those blessed medals that had been blessed each evening by our Lady were now even more precious to me. Thank you, Lord.

The final day, Father Isaac had been given the privilege of being the main celebrant for the English-speaking Mass. We were all excited to be participants in the Mass in Saint James. Imagine! My husband was the lector for the Scripture reading, my two children and Craig one by one read their own prayer petitions to the congregation, and I was responsible for taking the video. It was a day to remember for all of us, and the video I shall cherish always.

On our flight home, everyone was exhausted. Each of us had different beautiful stories to tell. Some in our group had seen the sun spinning and pulsating—I didn't. Others smelled roses. Some saw our Lady at the church door each morning; still others saw the cross illuminated at night or saw it disappear altogether (the villagers say when the cross disappears it is because our Lady is praying in front of it). I saw none of these things. I just felt a very strong peacefulness. I wanted to pray all of the time. My son said, "I never thought I could stay in church for five hours and not mind." I think he speaks for all of us. Prayer was always on our lips and in our hearts. Oh, if we could only bring Medjugorje home with us. If only others could experience this place and live the messages, our world would be almost perfect.

When we arrived back in the States, we all went back to our ordinary lives richer. Young Lowell's rosary turned a golden color the night we arrived home. He went on to share his experiences and display the rosary with his Dad at service clubs and businesses. Kim and Craig went home with their daughter Kalyn. Kim tried to start a rosary group in her little town in North Carolina—not too successfully, but she is still trying.

My husband, Lowell, began to witness and show the video to service organizations. We joined a rosary group of fellow Medjugorje travelers as well as a prayer group organized by Lowell's church.

Three months after our return my husband was diagnosed with lung cancer which had metastasized. He had never been sick a day in his life and had annual physicals. He died five months later. He was fifty-seven. Ah . . . but what he did with those five months! He never gave up. He turned himself over to our Lord with no bitterness and was an inspiration on the cancer floor to other patients. One night our rosary group came and prayed the rosary. The Medjugorje Ave Maria rang in the hospital corridor, bringing peace and joy to other patients. The nurses wept when Lowell died.

I did not know why we were called to Medjugorje, but I know now. Our family needed the deepening of our faith to enable us to accept Lowell's death. We needed to be enriched in the love of the Lord to sustain us, and sustain us it has!

Although Kim and I are miles apart, we both made a private decision to go through instructions to become Catholic. I think this was kindled by the love we felt for the Eucharist in Medjugorje.

It is said that in the beginning when God scattered stars into space, he planned treasures for us to discover—like love and life and people like Lowell. God took our treasure, but prepared us for the taking by inviting us to Medjugorje through the gentle urging of our Mother Mary. Because of Medjugorje, I know that someday I will be reunited with my Lowell, where we shall live again in God's beautiful presence for all eternity.

Dedicated to the memory of my husband, Lowell Lemmon

[Responding to the confusion of a Catholic priest over the cure of an Orthodox child (1984–85)]

*T*ell everyone that it is you who are divided on earth. The Muslims and the Orthodox, for the same reason as Catholics, are equal before my Son and me. You are all my children.

—Message given to visionaries by Mary, September 4, 1982

Mother of the Eucharist:
A Presbyterian Minister's
Perspective of Medjugorje

Steven Muse

I remember as a boy attending Mass at my Roman Catholic friend's church. I went up in single file to receive the Communion wafer like all the rest, grateful that I didn't get stopped and questioned in the line and feeling as though I had somehow gotten away with something I wasn't supposed to. Although at the time I didn't know all the theological ins and outs that separated us, I knew enough not to stand there and announce to the priest I was Presbyterian. Foremost in my mind was that we both loved Jesus as lord and savior, and that seemed to be what was important at the time, though I was vaguely aware that Protestants and Catholics were distinct in some way or another. If pressed to explain, I probably would have said the differences had to do more with the fact that *they* had statues of Mary in their sanctuary and a corpse hanging on the cross—strangely fascinating—while ours lacked both. *Our* pastor allowed us to attend their services while they weren't permitted to visit ours. It was only after I was ordained a Presbyterian minister that I became concerned with all the reasons why we weren't officially allowed to eat at one another's table. While the fires of my childhood naivete had been, by then, buried under the accumulations of academic theological scruples, they were never entirely extinguished, but continued smoldering like some phoenix ready to rise from its own ashes with healing in its wings.

Roman Catholics, Eastern Orthodox, and Reformed Christians accept the validity of one another's baptism. We unite on behalf of human hunger, poverty, and loneliness because we share a common human heart, a common home on the planet, and common limits of birth and space and time, suffering and death. We share creation in the image of a common God and the rain falls upon us all alike, whether just or unjust, Christian, Muslim, or Jew. How strange that when we come to the table of Eucharist (which means *thanksgiving*), the source of our gratitude becomes a dividing wall between us.

One minor epiphany occurred for me when a young Chinese engineer visiting with our family for the Christmas holidays attended worship. Her English was good, but she hadn't been with us long enough for me to realize how much of the nuances of our previous theological discussions had been lost on her in spite of her gracious smiles and timely nods. Before our traditional Christmas Eve Communion service, I explained the sacrament of the Lord's Supper as best I could, reiterating the part about how if you are not a baptized, professing Christian you *don't* partake. She indicated with a gracious smile that she had understood. After all, I thought, in the primitive church unbaptized Christians were not even permitted to be in the same room when prayers and Communion were celebrated. Furthermore, there was a mandatory three-year period of instruction and testing for catechumens before they were finally accepted. Of course, in those days Christians were laying their lives on the line every time they met, and the church could not take a chance on any counterfeits being allowed in to squeal on them. Still it had seemed appropriate to me to make this small request some two thousand years later because holy Communion was not something to be taken lightly. The Apostle Paul had written to the Corinthians that in fact there were some among his churches at the time who "had taken Communion unworthily and died" as a result (I Corinthians 11:30).

During the service when people came forward to receive the elements, I had a few seconds to decide how to deal with the fact that this unbaptized, untutored, admitted atheist was also making her way down the aisle to receive holy Communion! Could she have had a sudden conversion, I wondered? And who am I to judge anyway? More than likely she hadn't understood after all; a fact which I later confirmed. In her own methodical scientific way she was going to "experience" the Eucharist just as she said she had wanted to do with regular

Sunday morning worship. While hers was not a bold arrogant approach, but more that of a gentle, humble enquirer's heartfelt curiosity, I couldn't say that it was the faith of a Christian either, could I?

I began to wonder in those few seconds available to me as she moved down the aisle, "Hadn't Jesus offered himself to those who didn't understand what they (or he) were doing? Had he fed only those of the five thousand who understood the true meaning of the bread and fish they were receiving? Even his disciples hadn't understood at the time. And good Lord! on one occasion he gave life to a dead man who didn't even ask him, simply because he had taken pity on the young man's grieving widowed mother, for he was her only son! (Luke 7:12) What is the Eucharist anyway? Jesus said, 'When I be lifted up I will draw all people to myself.' Hadn't he intended this to come to pass?"

T he substance of all these considerations was never so clear to me as it became during the week I received him daily from the hand of the priests in the Church of Saint James in Medjugorje, Yugoslavia. There I found somewhat to my surprise, because I had received Eucharist hundreds of times in various Protestant churches over a lifetime, that my mouth became the door to my heart, and it was as if I had swallowed holy fire that seemed to rip the curtain of my academic filters in two, revealing my heart as a tabernacle of joyful sorrow for which I could only give thanks over and over, realizing that I was simultaneously incurring and being forgiven a debt far beyond anything I could ever repay. I certainly didn't deserve what I was being given. I had passed no tests that made me worthy. My God; by receiving the host as the flesh of Jesus Christ I was admitting his *real* presence, which served to confirm that I had also *really* helped crucify the man! This realization pressed deep into my heart like waves of grief, and I found myself embracing the mystery of it gratefully and of my own free will. It was clear to me that I could have stopped the experience at any moment by shifting my attention away from this center springing up out of some place I could not follow with my conscious mind, but I did not want to. I knew somehow that there was also in that grief the seeds of healing and joy if I were also willing to receive his forgiveness. To accept forgiveness meant, of course, that I would be admitting that I needed it. It would mean that I no longer belonged to myself, but had been bought with a price that I could never repay. And yet I knew the more deeply I realized this, the more I would want to. Everything that I am and possess would become part of him and belong to the world as he belongs to the world in his great unfathomable love. *His Father would become my Father and his Mother would become my Mother.* It was more than I could comprehend in words. My heart swelled within me, swallowing my mind and squeezing hot grateful tears out of closed eyes like great drops of blood. I had been drawn into this moment of eucharistic presence—the sacramental heart of the Christian mystery—by responding to the sweet gentle presence of the Virgin Mary, which at least in that place was almost palpable.

The *Mother of God.* I had come to respect her place in Christian tradition, even before I visited Medjugorje, through a growing appreciation for Greek Orthodoxy, which refers to her with the word *Theotokos,* which means literally "God-bearer." The Gospel begins with the joyful mystery of the Annunciation to the Virgin Mary of the Incarnation of God's love within her. If in Jesus Christ the divine Person became fully human (cf. John 1:1,14), then Mary is not simply the mother of a man only, but the Mother of God as well, for Christ is *fully human* and *fully God.* Only if he is God, can Mary be called "God-bearer"? If she is not, then he is not. If he is not, then she is not. They cannot be separated. There is no way to acknowledge this truth apart from acknowledging Mary as the mother of him in whom humanity is perfectly united with divinity. Thus in Jesus Christ, the Mother of God becomes the mother of us all who share the one body of Christ which is the church universal. Christian tradition is very clear about this and so was I, intellectually at least, but I did not yet feel the significance of it in my heart.

Something had begun to stir in me in this respect when my mother died, but my Presbyterian upbringing had not sufficiently prepared me to receive God's love associated with a feminine image, but when it happened, mingled with the same love I'd associated all my life with Jesus, it could not easily be dismissed.

My mother died in 1985 of the worst case of rheumatoid arthritis that Duke Medical Center has ever seen. She was by then, after a thirty-year siege with that demon, a sixty-five-pound shell of twisted aching bone and suppurating flesh hanging onto the last drop of life, because somewhere inside that crippled amputated body was a heart still without bitterness that wept with joy at the touch of a child's hand, laughed till she hurt at a good joke, and attracted the interest of all manner of people who found their way into the nursing home, because they sensed in her an appreciation for life and for *them*. When I poured her ashes into the ocean she loved, as she had asked me to do before she died, I realized strongly that the love I had for my earthly mother was somehow interwoven with a love for the Mother of God I had not allowed myself to give expression to. I had lost my biological father at age three and as a boy I had a vivid sense of having a Father in heaven, but my mother was still on earth. Somewhat inexplicably for a Protestant (although I am told Martin Luther did), I had begun praying the rosary a year or two earlier (before my mother's death) while running, so there was already forming in me a sense of having a Mother in heaven as well. Schubert's "Ave Maria" sung by Pavarotti was playing in my grandfather's apartment where I was staying on the day of the funeral service. I had never heard it before. My mother loved music more than anything, and my grandfather liked only opera. It came to represent for me a providential melding of many loves in my life from that day forth and still occasionally brings tears to my eyes when I hear it. I wrote in my journal what came to me that night when I stood knee deep in the waves saying good-bye to my earthly mother and had the words inscribed on the bottom of the old antique English writing box I had carried her ashes in:

I believe that suffering gives God opportunity to join flesh and spirit in Holy Wedlock which no power on earth or in heaven can put asunder. God risked life in the flesh in order that the flesh might have life in the Spirit. What I know of love I learned through my flesh.

Grief. Sadness. Joy. Only as I have experienced their tex-
ture in my body do I know their presence—as iron filings
reveal a magnetic field. The body is the doorway to eternity. Through it God prepares for the coming to birth of
his Holy Word out of nothingness. As I stood on the
shore and let mom's ashes slip through my fingers into
the waves I came to know that all human grief is one
grief—Mary weeping silently and helplessly before the
tragedy of her suffering son. And all joys are one joy—
the gladness of all the hosts of heaven praising and glori-
fying G_D Whose Word mysteriously gives life to all flesh
through the resurrection of Himself in Jesus Christ the
Son. That love comes to perfection through the free gift
of the fragile Creation to the desire of the Holy Spirit to
impregnate her. It is a mystery so ordinary as to be over-
looked and yet without the willingness of Mary who said,
"Let it be done to me according to Thy Word." God would
have had no mother and Creation no Savior. Truly we
may call her blessed, "Ave Maria."

When I returned home from North Carolina, I found my
rosary hanging on the bookcase where I always kept it in my
office. Oddly, the crucifix was missing from it. It had been
given to me by the priest at the local Catholic church to whom
I had gone to ask to teach me how to pray with it. It had one
arm missing, and I used to imagine in my mind that some day
that arm would grow back as a sign to me of the reality of God.
All that was left of it now was the center link with the image of
Mary on one side and the Apparition to the children at Fatima
on the other. I never found the crucifix. One part of me
explained the coincidence by thinking perhaps the cat had
pulled it off, although it had hung there in my office for years,
and in all that time I'd never seen the cat so much as notice it
hanging there some three feet off the ground. Another part of
me connected this "sign" with my mother's death and a dream
I'd had in seminary in which a voice said, "Why do you always
give everything to the Son? Why don't you give something to
the Mother?" It was one of the first dreams that caused me to
rethink my relationship with the feminine. I had "Ave Maria"
inscribed on the box that had carried my mother's ashes and

gave it to my wife to keep her treasures in and to signify that love is passed on from person to person forever.

By the time I arrived in Medjugorje I had begun praying the Jesus prayer and using a silent, imageless focus of attention on Christ as set forth within the context of Orthodox theology, and I had not prayed the rosary for six or seven years. Now here I was, a Protestant minister steeped in Eastern Orthodox spirituality, praying the rosary again in a Roman Catholic parish, and finding my heart turning inside out, calling me toward the one common denominator of all three—the Eucharist—like the hart longs for cooling streams. Once again after some twenty-five years I was standing in the Communion line to receive that tiny little wafer. Only this time there was no sense of getting away with anything. The mystery of Christ's eucharistic presence was quickened by the gift of faith that had by God's grace already weathered many a storm over the years and that was being made more *real* now by the reality of his Mother in our midst. Somehow the rightness of being there in that place, receiving that gift, seemed to have more to do with faith and God's grace, characterized by a mother's tender all-embracing love and a father's self-sacrifice, than with the form of church government or the legitimacy of any one denominational brand over another. And yet, I cannot say that these are insignificant either, for there is a cognitive dimension to faith; not any old belief will do. The fact remains that never before or since in my life have I had such an encounter with Christ in the Eucharist. I believe this is because I never received the bread and wine as the Body and Blood of Christ, so what I loved in my heart and believed with my mind were never experienced as real in the here and now of my bodily presence as I encountered him again and again for the entire week. Sometimes this happened twice a day as I received Communion both in the morning at English Mass, and again in the evening at the Croatian Mass where I did not even understand what they were saying or singing but only prayed the rosary in my own language with the others as if I had been saying "Hail Marys" all my life. What was true was that Father, Son, and Holy Spirit were real. And *Mary was real.*

Is it strange that I should have been led to the most profound encounter I have ever had with Jesus in the Eucharist by having responded to a call from Mary? Not really. I think how thousands have done the same thing in the Ukraine as well and increasingly as never before since the birth of Christ on every continent in the last fifty years due to the apparitions of the Blessed Virgin, who has said she is the mother of us all and loves each one of us no matter what our faith. Where there is Christian faith, her presence is a "eucharistic presence" that testifies to the fact of the incarnation, death, resurrection, and present reality of Jesus Christ and the Communion of Saints who intercede with us before God with their prayers. Wherever she appears and speaks with people, it is a clarion call to enter deeper into relationship with Jesus, who becomes flesh for us, again in the Eucharist. And if we pray for each other while on earth, how much more should we seek the prayers of those who are among the Communion of Saints with the Lord in the eternal present, sharing the same love God has for us? Millions are coming closer to Jesus because the Mother of God's invitation is moving them. This is not strange at all when we realize that, if there is no way to God, except through Jesus, then there can be no relationship with Jesus apart from one with Mary, who is the source of his humanity, for the startling claim of the New Testament is that Jesus Christ is *both* Son of God *and* Son of Man. In him, the Infinite Invisible Source of all that exists, whom no one has ever seen, took on flesh without diminishing himself, accepting limitation in every particular way that marks the human condition, including birth and mortality. It is a preposterous claim that flies in the face of reason and stretches the bounds of historical truth into the realm of myth while purporting to be fact. Jesus was executed for making such a claim about himself. Most of his apostles and thousands of those who joined them in calling Jesus "My Lord and my God!" suffered similarly for three hundred years afterward. Why?

The simplest explanation is that the first apostles saw Jesus in the flesh before the crucifixion, and then again afterward in his resurrected body, and from then on lived with a peace that passes human understanding even in the midst of terrific trials. Most of us will not have that privilege this side of death; yet the Gospels were written so that we might share that same apostolic faith. When Mary first appeared in Medjugorje she said, "I have come to tell you that God exists." For those who do not see her, she has said, "Let them believe as if they see me." Jesus said the same: "Blessed are you who believe these things without having seen." What kind of blessedness does this refer to? I am increasingly convinced that no miraculous sign happening outside of me can ever change me inwardly. Even if I were to see a man raised from the dead, there is a sense in which I would only become more fascinated by the mechanics of it, more interested in explaining it, still wondering what it all means, and never coming to saving faith. And yet if there is faith, then the most ordinary of encounters can reveal to us the most extraordinary of relationships. For me, staring into the sun, which appeared to be covered by a circular host, without hurting my eyes, at 1:30 in the afternoon, did not touch my heart so much as it engaged my speculative and scientific mind. I timed it on my watch and questioned those around me to see what was happening for them. But then receiving an ordinary little wheat wafer onto my tongue in the name of Jesus Christ and swallowing it left me weeping like a child in its mother's arms. There is no question in my mind which is the greater miracle: the visible sign or the faith that is present to interpret it to the heart under the inspiration of the Holy Spirit. And yet both are important, for together in the worshipping community, they signify the sacramental mystery of our faith—the meeting of heaven and earth in our lives that bears the fruit of love.

Christianity is first and foremost a faith in divine love that breaks forth into the joyful sorrow of Eucharist even when defeat seems most evident to the senses. Just as the Lord's Supper is more than merely eating and drinking, so faith in Christ is more than belief in the Resurrection. Both of these occur in a larger context whose character the church has been attempting to spell out in words for the last two thousand years, at times causing many to lose track of what is most essential, that is, the Word made flesh in our lives. As Saint Paul put it, "If I have prophetic powers, and understand all mysteries and all knowledge and if I have all faith, so as to remove mountains, but do not have love, I am nothing" (I Corinthians 13). Jesus was not the exclusivist. That was the Pharisees' special province. They were the ones building a religious country club. When Jesus' disciples played one-upmanship among themselves in a similar fashion, the savior put his arms around a child and declared, "Whoever receives one of these children in my name receives me and not me but him who sent me." Still jockeying for position sometime later, the disciples ask the Lord if they should forbid a group of people from casting out demons in Jesus' name, "because they are not following us" (Mark 9:38). The answer is clear: "No, whoever is not against us is for us." When Jesus accompanied Cleopas and the other disciple along the road hours after his Resurrection, and sat at table with them, he was still not making the kind of rigid distinctions we latter-day theologians often employ, not to show how all people by the grace of God are included in the body of Jesus Christ, but rather to insist on the ways by which they are excluded because of limitations of human comprehension of academic distinctions most people are no more aware of than I was when I first received Communion with my Roman Catholic friends as a young teenager. This does not mean that careful thought about what we believe is not warranted, or that we can dismiss the differences between the denominations as irrelevant. Not at all. What it means is that we must enter more deeply into them and into ourselves until we can see the universal implications of the particular that are the marks of the true Catholic faith. It also means, I think, that like the five wise blind men examining different parts of the elephant, we need each other to appreciate the whole picture . . . the marks of the true Catholic faith. Saint Ignatius in the first century after Jesus remarked, "Wherever the whole of Christ is, there is the Catholic church." Human beings are created in the image of God. Each person is unique and cannot be duplicated. The four Gospel writers saw the same Christ from unique perspectives, and we would be the poorer were we to lose even one of them. Could it be that the true Catholic Church, like Christ himself, has been in our midst from the very beginning and yet we have not seen? We have not seen that all people and the earth itself reveal the glory of God. The gift of Mary's presence and the simplicity of her message give me wonder about the nature of some of the distinctions we place in the minds of those whose simplicity would otherwise enable them to find Christ present in a thousand places ecclesiology fears to tread.

When my Chinese friend finally got to me, I served her from the cup of the New Testament in Jesus' blood that is poured out for the salvation of the world. I hope Jesus was pleased with what I did, just as I hope he is pleased with the graciousness of the Roman Catholic Church to serve me from its bounty and to allow me to enter through the wide open arms of my Mother in Heaven into the heart of the Christian mystery, which is the body of Jesus Christ, the church of all creation. I like to believe that in similar circumstances Jesus would have said to anyone who tried to refuse either of us Communion, "Let him who is without any confusion regarding the Sacrament of the Eucharist be the first to prevent them from receiving." Then afterward he would say to us all, "Did anyone stop you?" "No, Lord." "Neither do I. But go and learn what this means."

Surely, we spend our lives learning what Christ's love means, and we will never fully understand until we are carried into the heart of the Holy Trinity in the church triumphant. The important thing is that we *begin* again and again; all along the way to love one another as we ourselves have been loved, remembering that whatever happens to us, there is no power on earth or in heaven that can separate us from the love of God given to us through Jesus Christ our savior. It is quite apparent that through him we not only have a father but also a mother in heaven and brothers and sisters in all peoples everywhere and in all times. For all of us, with John, stand at the foot of the cross of Jesus, and standing there we receive Mary as our mother and John, and all the other disciples as our brothers and sisters, even as we receive Jesus our lord. This is very, very good news. It reminds me of one evening in January of 1991 around ten o'clock at night, standing beneath the cross in the darkness on Apparition Hill above the villages of Bijacovici and Medjugorje. A few candles are burning at the base of the cross. Many nationalities are represented: German, Italian, Yugoslavian, French, Hungarian, and English. The visionary Ivan and his prayer group are present singing familiar tunes with unfamiliar words in wonderful fresh Croatian diaphonic harmonies and syncopated rhythms. Soon groups begin to pray the rosary simultaneously, each in their own languages. At the signal all face the cross and become quiet while the apparition occurs. Bunching together in groups, at its conclusion we strain to hear the translation into our native tongues: "Mary came accompanied by three angels and prayed for peace. She blessed all the people and prayed over us with outstretched arms and blessed the religious articles we had brought with us, and she asked us to pray for peace." Sighs of joy sound the same in every language. More prayers and songs of gratitude—"Ave Maria" is sung in every language present with great tenderness by everyone assembled—quiet heartfelt sounds of praise and thanksgiving rising up like incense from beneath a vast star-pitted sky above, mirrored by the tiny pinpoint lights of the villages gleaming below. Turning to go down the rocky slope in the cool winter darkness, I do not know if I am in heaven or on earth. I believe this is the way God meant it to be.

Praised be Jesus and Mary!
Glory be to the Father and to the Son and to the Holy Spirit
as it was in the beginning, is now, and ever shall be
world without end.
Amen.

I *am giving you my special blessing. Carry it to every creature so that each one may have peace.*

—Message given to visionaries by Mary,
December 25, 1988

A Unitarian Universalist's Experience in Medjugorje

William M. Ames

I visited Medjugorje in May of 1991. I knew the experience would be an outstanding one, and I was not disappointed. Writing this chapter allowed me to revisit the memory of my trip, which is still in my mind at least once a day, and reminds me yet again of the powerful role that faith, hope, and prayer play in my life.

However, before I tell of my experience in Medjugorje, let me begin by focusing on myself and on some of the differences between Protestants (specifically Unitarians) and Catholics. We live in a far more liberal-minded age than the one in which our parents lived, and our children will also benefit from this trend toward a more live-and-let-live attitude. For me, my Protestant faith is very comfortable, and this faith was affirmed by my experiences at Medjugorje.

I was christened Unitarian in my sixteenth year and was given godparents. I had received instruction on Unitarianism and Christianity in general many years previously in Sunday school, and at the time of my christening, like all adolescent boys, I was far more concerned with sports, girls, and other secular activities than expanding my appreciation of the Unitarian faith.

The fact that Unitarians do not believe in the Trinity of the Father, the Son, and the Holy Spirit was not really apparent to me back then. I had no knowledge of other Christian faiths, so I also did not realize the real impact of the fact that to my fellow Unitarians Jesus was a prophet on the level of Moses and Buddha and nothing more. Certainly the concept of the Protestant heresy and its implications were well beyond my scope of thought. And the idea that the death and resurrection of Jesus deserves little more than the status of being just another holiday was not an issue for me.

An ancestor, William Ames, was one of the leading proponents of Puritanism in the early 1600s and, after he was expelled from England for his beliefs and had sailed to Holland, he wrote the landmark books and essays defining the Puritan movement.

Unitarian Universalism (UU from this point on), is an offshoot of the Puritan Revolution. Today, because of their "liberal" theology, UUs are frequently the object of derision from the followers of the more orthodox Protestant denominations, not to mention most Catholics. The church is accused of being a haven for people who cannot make up their minds; of walking the thin line between confusion and indecision; of not having crosses burned into our lawns by bigots, but rather question marks.

Unitarians are religious liberals who rely less on an institutional generated belief set and more on one generated from within. We have an eclectic system of theology that encourages each individual to develop a personal faith that is not dependent on the demands of an institution. Perhaps by today's standards my ancestor would have been a Unitarian. As a Puritan he deplored the excesses of the Anglican Church—especially the debauchery of the students he taught as the master of Cambridge University's Christ's Church College. He took his religion (and probably himself) very seriously, and he did not like to see it embellished or changed to suit the temper of the times. Historians say his exit from England was hastened by his disapproval of the surplice and other outward symbols that he viewed as irrelevant to his faith.

Despite my UU background, I have been attending Catholic Mass regularly over the last ten years since I moved to Cambridge, Massachusetts. When I lived in Boston, I had attended Episcopalian services at Trinity Church and occasionally a UU service. Being true to the eclectic nature of my home religion, I did not see a problem with attending services of other denominations.

Like most pilgrims, I came to Medjugorje to find and experience a deeper appreciation of God in my life. An interest in religion and going to church had been part of my life for a long time, but I had always assumed that there was a more than even chance that the Bible was filled with apocryphal stories—the inevitable result of centuries of interpretation, evaluation, and probably exaggeration.

My search for God originated in the pursuit of my interest in starting a business. A faith does not arise out of a vacuum or a life of ease, and certainly that has been the case for me. Ten years ago I worked in business as a security analyst for an investment management company. My view of my own future was that, if I wanted to succeed and make a name for myself, I would have to leave the investment business and strike out on my own. So I "stepped off the curb" in 1981 and I quit my job. Ten years later, and with help from numerous others, my business is almost started.

During the past ten years, despair has come upon me often, as there have been many disappointments. To cope with these seeming disasters, I often went to Saint Paul's Catholic Church to pray. Inevitably this prayer would raise my spirits, but as the years passed and the length of my journey seemed so long, so difficult, and without any sign of immediate or even intermediate gratification, I questioned my fate. But each time I left church, I just knew that God wanted me to keep trying. What exactly his plan for me was had escaped me, except that perhaps he had decided that I should lead a life of poverty. I read a quotation sometime back to the effect that those whom God loves, he tests with great hardship to see if their faith is true. That I could understand, but reading the lives of the saints revealed to me that time after time they felt a lack of faith or inadequacy in the eyes of the Lord. I was always aghast at the lack of faith professed by these most holy of people. I used to wonder to myself as I sat in a pew at Saint Paul's in the middle of the afternoon: How could I hope to attain a true faith and a state of grace in the eyes of the Lord when these people, these saints, felt inadequate?

In pursuit of all possible secular assistance to find God, I attended many self-help seminars in the eighties. EST was the one I remember best. They put a hundred people in a room and did their best to make them feel inadequate and then proceeded to give the group their formula for a successful life. Seemingly inspired by Sartre's famous dictum "Hell is

other people," this formula included techniques to manipu-
late other people, all the while couched in fairly rational and
selfless terminology. And in all fairness, EST undoubtedly
helped many people through difficult periods in their lives.
For me, however, EST felt too superficial to have much of a
lasting impact.

I was kidding myself if I ever believed that I had attained
any sort of a lasting faith. Then I went to Medjugorje. I went
as a tourist, became a pilgrim, and then saw the light (the
light being the sun dancing in the sky, which we all saw mid-
week during our stay). This felt as close to finding God as I
had ever been.

The stories of the pilgrims in Chaucer's *Canterbury Tales*
began to recur to me as our bus approached Medjugorje.
There really was such a thing as a pilgrimage, I remember
thinking. My group began to recite the rosary. I had no beads
of my own, and, even if I had, I did not know what the rosary
was all about, did not really know the words, and, most of all,
considered it a ritual that usually made me very uncomfortable. In my Protestant way, I had visions of priests leading con-
gregations in the rosary and at the same time passing the
plate for donations as the worshippers had become hypno-
tized by the constant repetition and consequently were willing
to give and give generously. The decades were led by our
group leader, Bernard. Bernie was a barber from Portsmouth,
New Hampshire, and, most of all, was a man of extensive
knowledge of Catholic history and practices. He had been to
Fatima and as our week progressed was able to interpret the
miracles of Medjugorje with a sensitivity and insight that continually pumped energy into our group and filled my week
with experiences I will never forget. Bernie quickly converted
me from tourist to pilgrim.

Next to me in the bus, intently saying the rosary, was my
Protestant friend Janet, who was directly responsible for my
being on the trip. Until about four years ago, she and her husband, Peter, had lived in my apartment building in Cambridge. After they moved, we had no contact until March when,
for no special reason other than to hear how they all were, I
called and spoke to Janet. It was a very fortuitous phone call.

When the subject of our vacations, past and future, came
up, Janet hesitatingly told me that she was going to Yugoslavia,

whereupon I asked her if she was going to Medjugorje. She was amazed that I knew of Medjugorje and quickly persuaded to me to come along after I told her that I had known of it for years and had recently been considering going there if I could find others who were interested. At her suggestion I called Bernard, who had been instructing her, and signed up for the trip.

As the rosary continued while we traveled the last few miles into Medjugorje, I felt a great sense of mystery and excitement about seeing the cathedral and the visionaries themselves. Probably like every one on that bus, I knew in my heart that coming to Medjugorje was the right thing to do. As a true Christian one must seek and not just sit around waiting. I just did not have any idea of what was going to happen to me. Would I be disappointed? Either way, at forty-seven years of age, the prospect of the unknown, of a surprise that could alter my life, was very exciting.

After we arrived and unpacked, a group of us walked into the town to Saint James Church. The building was crowded and the six o'clock prayers had already begun. So we worked our way through the crowd along the side aisle up to the front to join the crowd near the altar area. My friend, "Pilgrim Janet," as I came to call her, found a key spot and we followed her. After kneeling to give thanks that I had made the decision to come to Medjugorje, I felt for the first time the power of this most incredible place.

I had never before seen such intensity in a church. As I had expected, there was a seriousness to the place that far exceeded the Sunday services I was used to back home. But there was also much more. As I looked out across the crowd and saw hope shining in the eyes of all the people, and felt the strong sense of faith in the words and in the soaring cadences of the songs and of the prayers, I began to sense the enormity of what Medjugorje was to the world. The cumulative impact of ten years of apparitions and the pilgrimages of twenty million people has caused a revolution among the Catholic clergy and laity.

The hope I felt in their presence and heard in the voices that evening was for peace, and that is what I discovered the message of Medjugorje to be. It took me several days to appreciate what is meant by *peace*. Peace within oneself leads to peace in families, which, thereafter, like the ripples created by a rock thrown into a small pond, can spread into every corner of the universe if that rock, the rock of our faith, is strong and large enough. Prayer and love are the bulwarks to our faith and to this peace.

As the service continued, despite not having slept for the previous twenty-four hours, my mind was empty of extraneous thoughts as the choruses of "Ave Maria" were sung out over and over again by my fellow pilgrims, other pilgrims of many nationalities and numerous Christian faiths. After I had heard its sound reverberate throughout Saint James Church and into my heart, for the first time in my life I knew there was a living God. Any lingering intellectual doubts disappeared like the early morning mist evaporates off a field.

At 6:40 the moment of silence for the apparition began and (please forgive my lyrical prose) I was in a state of wonder. To think that the Virgin Mary was then appearing to the visionaries in the balcony behind us is beyond description. It changed my life forever and in ways that I am still discovering many months later! The service continued for the next two hours, and I must admit, while it was hard for me to fully grasp the meaning of the presence of the Holy Mother in our midst, it was also hard to kneel for all the prayers. I left that night with sore knees and felt both mentally and physically exhausted from the experience.

At dinner I started to understand what a pilgrimage was all about. For the first time in my life I was in a discussion about my own faith and was describing it without my usual apologetic posture for my UU faith. No question that being a Unitarian makes one a curiosity—some of my fellow pilgrims found it very ironic that they had met for the first time a genuine Unitarian in this most holy of places. Here was somebody whose official organized faith did not necessarily believe in Jesus as the one true Christ and to whom the Virgin Mary was little more than a major supporting character in the biblical story.

But the question put to me was: "In what do you believe?" People asked if I shared the UU point of view about these seemingly agnostic beliefs. I tried to articulate the idea that within UU people can create their own beliefs based solely on a belief in one God. We believe in Johnny Appleseed, E. E. Cummings, and many others, if not as prophets then as spiritual leaders. Issues of the Trinity, the death and resurrection of Jesus, and so forth, are left up to the individuals to decide for themselves.

The story of the early days of Medjugorje contains particularly compelling imagery for a Protestant. In the first week back in June of 1981, before the Holy Mother and the visionaries agreed to meet in the church, Mary would appear to them at the foot of the hill where a large crowd gathered to witness this happening. The people passed by the church on the way to the hill. The building was empty, and the priest, Father Jozo, must have felt quite useless as the people went to witness Mary speaking directly to the visionaries, and thus to the people. There was no need for a priest in this situation. Who needs to read a newspaper if there is easy access to the primary source?

Eventually, of course, the situation became so difficult that Father Jozo and other church members decided upon the current formula where the apparitions take place in the church at 6:40 P.M. (5:40 P.M. in the winter), and all worshippers therefore are witnesses, as the apparitions and the Mass take place in the same building.

The fact that the clergy were bypassed by the people on their way to meet or to be in the presence of Mary may be of little or no interest to Catholics, because they see the clergy as playing a key and an inevitable role in interpreting the word of the Lord. But many UUs believe that there is no fixed belief set that accompanies the role of pastor. No institution, person, or priest can act as the interpreter of the word of God to others.

Therein lies my basic reaction to the Medjugorje experience. In my view, the Lord has spoken to me via the Virgin Mary through the visionaries, and that is all that matters. The man who translated for Ivan was not a priest but a friend of his family. When we questioned him, we did not go through a member of the clergy who was aware of every subtle shade of doctrine and consciously or unconsciously projected that to us and to Ivan.

It was a refreshing sight to see in the crowd at Ivan's house many priests listening to the lay people describing and relaying the word of the Virgin Mother. We were not in a crowded cathedral, but in a farmyard. Behind us was the stable with the farm animals and the machinery, and in front of us was Ivan's family home.

This is a scene in which Jesus must have stood many times during his ministry. Personally, I think it is very hard for the doctrines of peace and justice to be adequately or convincingly preached inside a massive building with ornate windows when so many are starving. They are unconscious reminders, regardless of denomination or faith, of the vested interest in a particular belief set that spends money on things instead of people. While buildings and surplices are inevitable (and here is my point), the "less is more" credo is a very loud and clear message when seen and heard in a farmyard in Medjugorje.

Since I am an enthusiast of the services at the Cathedral of Saint Paul, I must admit that I am also talking out of both sides of my mouth. After all, those farmyards can get more than a little chilly and damp in the middle of the winter. And a service with plenty of music from a well-rehearsed choir can be a lot more pleasant than the braying of farm animals.

My only other point merely echoes that of my Protestant faith—that people who put their faith in institutions often end up cynical and disappointed. That is the Protestant heresy: Self-reliance and charity are the only pathways to personal salvation, and organized religion must be approached from these vantage points. That is what I believe, and in the Medjugorje experience it was affirmed for me and in me. (Pilgrim Janet clearly disagreed with my assessment, and last Sunday I attended her conversion mass.)

I did see the sun dance in the sky. On the way to breakfast on Wednesday, my fellow pilgrims Kay and Priscilla called me over to look at the sun and there it was—dancing in the sky. What more could I ask for?

*The Mount Krizevac cross stands as a monument to the
courage, tenacity, and devotion of the local villagers.*

Saint James Church.

Local residents gather outside Saint James Church after Mass.

Vicka welcomes pilgrims outside her home.

The cross on the Hill of Apparitions is the focal point of the late evening apparitions.

Ivan speaks to a crowd gathered outside his home. Interpreter, Iliana, translates for English-speaking pilgrims.

On December 28, 1989, atop the Hill of Apparitions, our Lady appeared to the visionaries. Upon leaving, she said she had left a gold cross in the sky and that it said "Glory Be to God in the Highest."

Chrissy Washburn lights her chalice on Mount Krizevac.

One of the bronze plaques that depict the Stations of the Cross along the path on Mount Krizevac.

*Statue of the Virgin Mary located in
Father Jozo's previous parish church.*

The cross on Mount Krizevac at sunset.

*G*od *has chosen each one of you in order
to use you in a great plan for the
salvation of mankind.*

—Message given to visionaries by Mary,
January 25, 1987

A Unitarian Universalist's Experience in Medjugorje

Christine Washburn

I t is interesting to me how life can take little twists and turns, some that affect you little, and some that have a never-ending and powerful impact on who you are and where you are going. And sometimes the twists that seem to have the greatest impact, others do not even notice. Last January I made a choice that offered me an experience so life affirming that its powerful impact is never ending.

I decided to join a group of people going on a religious retreat to Medjugorje, Yugoslavia. The reason I joined this group was to earn three hours of theology credit required for my master's degree at Loyola College. At the time I signed up for this retreat, I had no idea what was happening in Medjugorje. I learned that ten years ago, six children were walking up the hill near their home in Medjugorje when an apparition of the Virgin Mary appeared to them. She repeated her visits and began speaking to them, bringing messages on how to find peace in the world. Although the children were not taken seriously those first few days, their devotion and commitment changed their own behavior such that the adults around them took notice and began to listen. The children, who are now adults, are called visionaries, and they have committed their lives to Mary's messages. A few of them are still blessed with the apparitions of Mary on a daily basis. The entire village of Medjugorje has been converted to living the messages from Mary. It has been a phenomenal occurrence.

When I read about the apparitions, I was impressed by the struggles that the visionary children, the adults in their lives, and the entire village have had to face. It is impossible to imagine these people operating their lives in the midst of such havoc and political challenge unless they believed with all their hearts that the apparitions of Mary are true. The villagers and visitors have experienced many different miracles. But apparitions and miracles are not things in which I believe. I had my doubts about it all. I even had some doubts about whether this religious adventure was something that would benefit me. You see, I am a Unitarian Universalist. UUs do not fall into the category of Christian religions. Since most of you reading this probably do not know about my religion, I need to take a few paragraphs to explain.

I hesitate, now, as I begin to tell you what Unitarian Universalism is all about, because inherent in our religion is the freedom for each UU to say what this religion means. Therefore, I am speaking only for myself and not for my church or any other UU. Other UUs would surely have ideas similar to my own in ways, but many would also differ in many other ways.

As a UU I have grown up believing that there are no "right" answers to the big questions we have about life, creation, God, the meaning of life, and death. I believe that we must follow our own paths, ask questions, gather information, call on the wisdom of others, and then put it all together and make some sense of it by ourselves. It is a time-consuming process that continues forever, with no absolute answers. There are times along this religious journey when I have felt at peace with my beliefs as if I had answers for me. But there have been other times when I have been confused and frustrated.

Our religion grew from the Judeo-Christian faiths, with our histories very much overlapping and moving together, although we entered the picture a little later. It was not until the early 1500s that the forerunners of UU began questioning the absolute truth of the Bible, the divinity of Jesus, the essence of God, and the hereafter. I would claim those so-called heretics as UU thinkers. UUs often pull away from traditional beliefs and reserve the right to explore ideas from new and different perspectives and come to new conclusions.

At my present old/young age of forty-five, I do have some conclusions with which I am comfortable. They include a strong belief in a positive force in this world. It is a force that holds us together and keeps our world in balance. This force is bigger and stronger than life as we know it on this planet. It is what makes love and good things happen. It is my concept of God, and I think it resides in every living and nonliving thing in this world.

There is also an evil force in the world. It has power and also resides in every living and nonliving thing. It is the force that makes negative things happen. It breeds hate. It influences us all at different times.

But I believe that most people are more influenced by the God within than they are by the evil within. We feed our God side by doing good things and loving others. We feed the evil force by doing bad things and hating others. My life experience has shown me that most people are busy trying to do good and love others most of the time.

My beliefs about Jesus are quite different from most of my UU friends, probably because of a very positive and loving experience I had when I was five years old. I attended a Baptist summer Bible school, and it was there that a warm and loving woman told me about Jesus. She said that Jesus was always on my shoulder. He loved me and he would always be there to help me. When I turned to see Jesus sitting on my shoulder, this kind teacher laughed and told me that I could not see Jesus, but he was always there. I believed her. The stories I heard about Jesus through the years created an ideal for me, a person for me to try to emulate. He was a person with ideas about how to love all others and how to live with people in peace. So I have a very strong attachment to Jesus. My visions of who he was and how he tried to live in the world guide me in my own life.

My beliefs about death are centered around reincarnation ideas. I like the idea that we have a mission in this life. Our next life will offer us another opportunity to learn new things or fix what we did not do so well in this life. This inspires me to want to get the most out of this life that I can, to learn and grow from my mistakes. I find great comfort in believing that it does not all end when we die. Our spirit will move on.

The little that I have studied of other religions leads me to believe that at base we are very similar. We all pretty much believe in living by the Golden Rule, doing unto others as we would have them do unto us. If we could all live by that rule more often, there would be more peace in our world. It is rather simplistic, I realize, but it inspires me and gives direction and meaning to my life.

So, with these liberal and unorthodox beliefs, I joined twenty-nine Catholics, three Lutherans, and a Presbyterian for ten days in a foreign country to experience this little village in the countryside of Yugoslavia. This was my first trip abroad and the first time that I was not frightened by the idea of leaving the safety of my own country, even though war with Iraq was an imminent possibility.

We arrived in Medjugorje very late at night after traveling for twenty-four hours. My first view of the village was early the next morning when I went for my daily run. I was struck by the simplicity of the place. It was hard to believe that it was here that twenty million people have visited in the past few years. It did not seem to have the accommodations and amenities that would be necessary for that many visitors. But, as I was soon to find out, the amenities to which I have grown accustomed in the United States are not all that necessary to daily life.

After our small group met together for our morning meditation and breakfast, we were all eager to visit the church Mary visits every day at 5:40 P.M. in the winter (6:40 P.M. in the summer). As I looked upon the church for the first time, this church where so much has happened and so many people have traveled miles to see, I did not see anything that was awesome to me. It certainly was not spectacular looking. I guess my first words to myself were, "What is the big deal here?" Obviously, I had lapsed into my more doubtful mode, questioning the reality of all the stories I had heard.

Once I was inside the church, I was not very impressed either. It was cold, dark, and uncomfortable. The ceiling was high and I felt small and insignificant. The words that were being spoken and the messages I was hearing were foreign to me. The worship and the ritual were troublesome to me. In fact, at this point, I wanted to be anywhere but where I was. I could hardly wait to be out in the sunlight again breathing fresh air.

I did try attending the church service a few more times with our group, since this seemed to be the way many of the people were finding their meaning. I did not want to jump to conclusions too quickly and perhaps lose out on something valuable. But, the experience inside the church did not grow on me in a positive way. When I was in the church I felt closed down and trapped. The places where I have always been able to feel the power of God are places where I feel the natural beauty of the world. I need a church with lots of windows that bring in the outside world. I need a place where I can feel free, not bound by too many rules or too much of the same thing. I need to hear new ideas and new ways of expressing those ideas and beliefs. I need symbols of life, hope, and joy. I need music with words that speak to me. Not only was all this missing, but I was constantly aware of the crucifix. It has always been very difficult for me to be in the presence of a crucifix, because when I look at it I feel death, destruction, despair, and depression. And so, this famous and inspiring church in Medjugorje was not inspiring for me. I needed to find another place to worship. Fortunately, it happened soon.

On our first day in the village we all walked a little more than a mile to Apparition Hill. This was the very same hill where the six visionary children first saw the apparition of Mary. We climbed up to the special places where Mary appeared. It was a fairly steep, rocky climb, and slippery with wet mud. But it was worth every treacherous step. With each step as we went higher, the simple valley farms below became more picturesque. By the time we were halfway to the top, we could see the entire valley before us with the church and the little village in the background. To me it was like a perfectly painted picture. While we listened to the church bells ringing, the roosters crowing, and the dogs barking, we looked up at the mountains and the sky around us. I could smell the clean, fresh country air. I could feel some safe loving spirit around me. Now this was a place where I could spend hours thinking and reflecting on life. I knew instantly where I would spend the majority of my time over the next week. This was the church for me. I was inspired by the beauty and the simpleness of it all. I was touched.

There was only one small problem with my newfound church place. I had to find the way there by myself. For many of you this may not sound like a large obstacle to overcome, but for someone like me, who can get lost going around the block, this was a frightening venture. Apparition Hill was about a mile and a half from where I was staying, and the route there was anything but straight and direct. The path went through the little village (no street signs), through farm fields (no directional signs), and through a small housing area. There were paths and streets of course, but they intersected and turned and split off from each other so that it seemed like a very complicated maze to me. The reason I can get so lost going around the block is because I totally lose my sense of direction after the first turn.

It was funny to me that, even knowing how lost I can get, I did not even think twice about the fact that I was going to find my way to the spot I had chosen. And the next morning, when I ran to Apparition Hill, it was almost like something or someone was there leading me. I did not get lost. I suppose it depends on your definition of miracles, but in my life, this could come close to one. When I reached my favorite spot on the top of the hill, I found a place to sit with the beautiful little peaceful valley in front of me. I felt special. I felt safe and protected. I have believed in the loving force of God for years, and I have felt the presence of that force at many different times in my life. Well, sitting on the rocks at the top of this small hill in Medjugorje, I felt the presence of that safe and loving spirit. I could not see it, or smell it, or hear it, but I know I felt it. Even though it was damp and cold and the sweat from my run was beginning to turn icy, I felt warm all over and there was a smile on my face that would not go away. That was day two of my adventure and it provided a real "high" for me.

Each morning from then on around 6:00 A.M. as dawn broke, I ran to the first cross on Apparition Hill. It was my very special way of saying good morning to God, to life. I know God's spirit was with me there. When most of my group attended church, which was often twice a day, I would walk again to Apparition Hill. It was there that I tried to make sense of what I was experiencing. There were many messages and many discussions that I was hearing that I needed to process and think about. That place on the hill inspired me. Each day I felt a little more sure of myself and my purpose for being on this trip.

One especially powerful experience for me on the hill occurred at 10:00 P.M. when Mary appeared to Ivan, one of the visionary children who still visits with Mary on a daily basis. With only our flashlights and the stars to aid us, about one hundred people climbed across the slippery, muddy rocks to the spot where Mary was to appear. There were many candles burning at the different crosses on the hill, flickering and providing a glow and warmth for all coming on the scene. I found a spot to sit, removed from the group. I wanted to witness this alone. Although Mary did appear to Ivan (we were told much later), I did not notice anything unusual. There was no special energy or safe feeling like I often had on the hill by myself. But what moved me was watching so many people from many different countries speaking different languages; watching people huddle together, all ages from two to ninety-two; listening to them pray together, praying for peace in the world. We were all unaware of the chilly, damp night air and the uncomfortable dirty rocks on which we were sitting. We were unaware of our differences. We were speaking as one and all wishing or praying for the same thing—*peace in the world.* Tears came to my eyes and goose bumps covered my arms. This is what it could be like all over the world. My belief that there can be peace among all people, without war, was being affirmed at this moment.

Coming down the mountain offered me another inspiring moment. It was late and dark and difficult to negotiate the slippery rocks. On most of the path, there was only room to descend in single file. Passing was extremely difficult to negotiate. In front of me at one point, there was a very elderly priest (I later found out that he was ninety-two years old). On either side of him, holding his arm and attempting to keep him from taking a spill, were two teenage boys, I would have guessed seventeen or eighteen years old, who somehow managed to negotiate the rocky sides of the path to take care of this special man. I was touched by their concern and their determination that nothing would happen to him. If he had taken a spill, I am sure they both would have flung themselves down to cushion his fall. That kind of human caring was heartwarming, and it seemed to happen often in this little village.

A few of the visionaries have committed their lives to sharing Mary's messages. They do this in many ways, one of which is to meet with groups of people to answer questions. On our second day we walked a mile or so to Ivan's house. He stood in his backyard with a translator and patiently answered the questions I am sure he has heard thousands of times. It was easy for me to be impressed by this young man whose commitment and devotion were so complete. He does not take money for his time, he simply asks for people to hear Mary's messages and begin to live by them. He was clear. He was calm. He was sure. He was unaffected.

The messages from Mary of which he spoke were centered around fasting, conversion, confession, and praying. These concepts are not part of my life beliefs. They sounded so Catholic. One of my biggest questions concerned the inclusiveness of these messages. Were they only for Catholics? Were they only for Christians? I asked Ivan how Mary speaks to non-Christians. Ivan said, "The Virgin Mother speaks to all people to pray for peace." Then I asked him if it mattered how people prayed or what they said in their prayers. Ivan answered, "Just pray for peace." I needed to know that this was a universal plea to all people, and that there were many different ways of accomplishing it. I had my answer.

On day three, we saw Vicka, another one of the visionaries. She was very different from Ivan in that she bubbled with enthusiasm. She said more about the messages of Mary. She told us that Mary is telling us that we need to turn off the TV because it is keeping us from paying attention to our real values and it is keeping us from being with each other. We must pay more attention to our family and our beliefs than we do to our cars and our things. She told us that Mary thinks of fasting as more than just giving up food for a day, but as an opportunity for us to give up some things in our life that are not good for us or for the world, like smoking, drinking, or lavish spending. It was easy to see the value in these words and messages.

The reason I had some problems with many of the messages I was hearing is because I have not been exposed to Christian ritual and ideas, nor have I been exposed to the Bible. There were times when I felt people were speaking another language. For instance, I had no idea what the Eucharist was. Communion was a new concept for me. The rosary prayers and peoples' discipline in saying them were a marvel. I had never heard of the Stations of the Cross before. And I struggle with the idea of prayer. *Fasting, confession, conversion,* and *repentance* are not words that I hear in my church. These are not concepts that are a part of my belief system. So, it took a major effort and some letting go for me to incorporate what was being said all around me. I had to incorporate the messages somehow to fit my beliefs.

On the fourth day in Medjugorje, we all climbed Mount Krizevac. At the top of this mountain there is a cross that can be seen from all around the little village. It is a magnificent sight. The story of how the cross was carried to the top of this mountain is inspiring. It was carried on the backs of people whose spirit was so stirred that they could accomplish the unbelievable. It was a remarkable feat, one that impressed me even more after my own climb up the mountain with only a little backpack.

The climb up Mount Krizevac is much steeper, rockier, and longer than the one to Apparition Hill. It takes about two hours to climb the mountain, partly because of all the stops along the way. There are fifteen special places to stop, each one depicting a part of the story of Jesus' crucifixion. The stops are the fourteen Stations of the Cross, and each is memorialized with a bronze carving of Jesus as he might have been seen at that moment so long ago. Our group stopped at each station to read the story and say a prayer. It was a wonderful learning experience for me because I had never heard the story of Jesus' crucifixion.

At the top of the mountain, when we finally arrived, I experienced the most magnificent view I have ever seen. I feel inadequate trying to describe the luscious scenes, or to describe my feelings. It was overwhelming. I have been on the top of other mountains and had similar feelings and been equally impressed with the spectacular views. But there was something special about this experience. I think it had something to do with my purpose for being there. It also had something to do with the purpose behind this climb for everyone. People were not climbing this mountain for the spectacular view. They were climbing it to feel closer to their God. They were looking for peace. They were finding both.

But the more significant climb up this steep rocky mountain was two days later when I went by myself. I had a burning desire to go up the mountain and do it my way, sending my messages out to the world, telling my story, saying my prayers. It is hard to describe the feeling I had as I set off that morning for my own private spiritual adventure up the mountain. There seemed to be an extra skip in my step and a smile on my face all the way. I felt like I was on a very important mission, one that only I could accomplish. With this simple climb, I was going to make a difference in the world, and it was a difference that only I could make. I felt very special. I was aglow.

I stopped at each station. I found a very special place to sit, with the cross behind me and the valley below filling the view in front of me. I had my chalice with me. The chalice is a symbol for Unitarian Universalism and holds a similar power for me as the symbol of the cross does for many Christians. The chalice stands for truth, hope, and freedom. Many of our churches light the chalice every Sunday. For me it is a very special ritual that bonds me with my faith and all others that participate in that ritual. I love it.

And so, it was with great pride that I took my chalice out at every Station of the Cross and lit it for peace in the world. I sat and soaked in the beauty around me. I felt the air and the forces that travel through it. I thought about things, ideas, and people that were important to me. I wished for good things to happen. I gave thanks for the wonders in the world, and in my life. I would just "be" and let my mind wander or go completely blank.

Each station was unique. The rocks and the vegetation around the stations made it a bit of a project each time I tried to find my place "to be." When I would finally choose my spot, I would look down on the valley below. Each time it was more beautiful. Because I was a little higher at each stop, the view was different every time. The valley seemed to expand and the details became more and more miniature. It almost seemed unreal, like a beautiful illustration in a fairy-tale book. Finding a stable flat place for my chalice was always a challenge, and on a number of occasions I wondered about its safety.

This particular chalice is very special to me. It was a gift from my church. I spent a year of special service helping to run our Religious Education (RE) Department while we were searching for a new RE Director. The chalice was handmade by one of the members in our church, and to me it is the most beautiful chalice in the world. It holds a place of honor in our home in the middle of the mantle over our beloved fireplace in the living room.

As I continued up the mountain, I felt continually washed over by a feeling of peace and contentment. I had a trust in this place. There was something unique going on here, and I was treasuring my being a part of it.

About two stations away from the very top of the mountain, I was again settling into a place for my own private worship and preparing to light my chalice. Suddenly my attention was diverted by a friend walking up the path just below me. I accidentally and carelessly knocked my chalice over. I let out a yelp. In that split second a million thoughts went through my brain. It was much like the stories you hear from people who have been in near-death experiences. I thought of all the memories that came with that chalice and the love I had for it. I felt the pain in my stomach as I saw it fall over the rocks and begin tumbling and crashing on all the rocks below. I felt myself move, faster than a speeding bullet and at the same time in slow motion, to reach out and save it from the death it would surely suffer if not caught. I was sick.

When I finally found the courage and the strength to move my body and assess the damage, I think I may have experienced my most precious and private little miracle. My chalice was not destroyed. Yes, there were two little chips out of the base, but it would stand just as sturdy and straight as before. I was overwhelmed with a feeling of relief. Looking down at the rocky path where it had fallen, it was unbelievable to me that it could have survived.

It was impossible for me to ignore this event as just a happening with no meaning. I believe this was significant. I searched for the next couple of days for the special messages this was trying to bring to me. I believe in the positive loving energy of God in the world, and that it has ways of communicating to us if we want to listen. I thought this was a time for me to listen carefully. There was a part of me that wondered if this was a message from the spirit of Mary telling me that I was devoted to the wrong religion, and I must now turn to the

Christian faith for my spiritual strength. However, that possibility remained in my head for only a matter of moments.

There is not one ounce of my soul that believes any loving spirit or God would claim one religion over another as superior. I believe that in our diversity and in our differences we can find great strength and beauty. What I experienced all week that had such power for me was the coming together of people from all over the world to pray together for peace in the world. Never did I feel or hear that there was only one right way to do that. What I saw in Medjugorje was the possibility that we can be of one purpose. Despite our differences, there are enough people on this meager little planet who want peace among all people that we could pull together and make it happen. I found a hope that I had never felt before.

So the message I heard as a result of my chalice falling affirmed everything I believed when I began this trip. The good loving forces in the world are more powerful than the evil and hateful forces. Yes, they can be knocked down, rolled around, and broken. They might be overwhelmed at times, seemingly beaten. But, they cannot be destroyed. They will always come out standing straight and firm. The loving forces of God in the world will survive and will be triumphant.

All of the messages I had been reading and hearing about during the week came together for me at that point. The essence of it is that we must put more effort into living our faith, whatever it is. The future of our world depends on us all giving a little more to each other, and using up our environment a little less. The Loving Spirit that holds our world in balance needs some help from us. From this day forward, I was determined to do more for others and use up less from our environment. This is not a whole lot different from how I think I have led my life so far. But somehow it felt so "right." Doubts that I have had periodically seemed to slip away. I do make a difference in this world no matter how large or how small the good deeds I do. And everyone else in this world makes a difference too.

Is Mary really appearing in Medjugorje? *I* would not call the presence the Virgin Mother. But yes, I do think there is some special loving spirit in this little village that is calling people to come there. When people come, they are touched by it. They are filled up, renewed, affirmed, inspired. I certainly was.

Is there something special about this little village of Medjugorje? Actually, that is hard for me to answer because it is the first little village I've ever seen outside our country. I loved the simple lifestyle. I loved being in a place that did not have the American materialistic emphasis. I loved having to live without some of my usual creature comforts. I loved watching the people pick their dinner from the fields. I loved watching people work more with their hands than with big fancy machines. I guess that could be found in lots of other little villages around the world. What makes Medjugorje special to me is how the people have responded to the event that has caused so much attention. They want to share their church, their hills and mountains, and their village. They want to share the peace and love and goodwill that they are receiving through their faith and their church.

Is this the only place in the world where a person can go and be touched by a special spirit and have a life-changing experience? No, I do not think so. I have had similar feelings at other places in our country where I joined groups in a spiritual growth kind of retreat.

I believe that part of the power of this experience comes from the beauty and natural state of the land there. Part of the power comes from the people I was with and our mutual caring and sharing with each other. Part of the power comes from that part of me that is open to experiencing it. And part of that power comes from the God source that I believe in. God was definitely present for me in Medjugorje. It all adds up to a life-changing experience and one that can pretty much happen anywhere, even in my own backyard. But, Medjugorje is a place where it all might happen a little easier.

So, am I really changed? My thirteen-year-old daughter's first question to me, asked with some trepidation, was, "Mom, are you all converted and different?" My response was, "No, Abby, I'm not all converted and different, at least not such that you'll notice any big change. But, yes Abby, I am converted and different. I have a stronger feeling of faith in my beliefs and my hope for the world. I feel more determined and able to give more and use less. I feel more at peace and more content. You probably won't notice much difference, but I do."

*Q uestion to Mary from visionary:
Are all religions good?*

*A nswer from Mary:
Members of all faiths are equal before
God. God rules over each faith just like a
sovereign over his kingdom.*

—Message given to visionaries by Mary,
October 1, 1981

An Episcopalian Catholic/ Roman Catholic Perspective of Medjugorje

Gay Lutton

W hen I made the decision to go to Medjugorje I had no idea why I wanted to go. I only knew that God was calling to me and that my yes brought me a great sense of peace.

I had no idea how I would get there. I did not want to make the travel arrangements because I am not a detail person and I really dislike that sort of thing. And anyway, it was not exactly like booking a trip to a Club Med somewhere in the islands. As far as I knew, not always being a politically well-read person, Yugoslavia was still a repressed communist country. This seemed to pose some problems that I was not willing to sort out on my own. Although my friend Peggy, who is very good at detail work, had agreed to go with me, we were too busy pursuing a master's in Pastoral Counseling at Loyola College to really get this trip off the ground. The spirit was most willing, but the flesh was weak! So I offered a prayer to God. "Dear God, if you really want me to go to Medjugorje then you had better drop this into my lap, because otherwise I'm afraid this just won't happen." That was in February of 1990.

My prayer was also a way of asking for another confirmation of the call I felt. Logically it did not make sense for me to go. Although I practice my belief in God in the Roman Catholic tradition, I have never had any devotion to the Mother of Jesus. I have always admired and respected Mary for her openness and her willingness to follow God's call, but I have rarely prayed to her as one of the Saints in either the Catholic or the Episcopal traditions. So why did that little inner voice keep telling me that going to Medjugorje was somehow right and good? Was I really being called to go there?

Toward the end of March 1990 there appeared on the bulletin board at school a notice. Loyola was offering a pilgrimage to Medjugorje. The trip was scheduled for January of 1991 during the Christmas break. They would take care of all the travel and housing arrangements. All I had to do was sign my name to the notice if I was interested. As I signed my name, I had to laugh. Be careful what you pray for, I thought, or you can find yourself traveling eight thousand miles to Yugoslavia in the middle of winter!

The January 4 entry into my travel journal describes the journey there. "Because of my 'yes' to God, I am now flying at 33,000 feet above the earth in a jumbo 747 Pan American jet on my way to Germany. It is 10:30 P.M. We are waiting for dinner to be served. Tomorrow we will land in Frankfurt and then fly on to Dubrovnik, Yugoslavia. From there we take a bus into the mountains—a three-hour trek along the sea, I understand. This is definitely not a journey for those with a weak faith!" We arrived after dark twenty hours later during a cold, driving rainstorm.

Martin, our host, his wife, and his sister greeted us (thirty-three in number) with a hot meal. Half of us stayed with his family in a hospitality wing they had built onto their two-story concrete, adobe house. The other half of our group stayed with Martin's neighbor in a similar accommodation. Our rooms were cold, as they do not turn the individual heaters on until their guests arrive in order to save money on electricity. Illeyana, our guide from the village, told us that during the early years of the apparitions when the Communists wanted to harass the villagers and pilgrims, they would turn the electric or the water off for several hours a day. We were grateful that no longer happens!

Medjugorje is a remote, mountain village area about one hour inland from the Adriatic Sea. Before the apparitions began, the population was made up of just a couple of hundred families who farmed the land. They did not have indoor plumbing or other amenities such as central heat or air-conditioning. There were few cars and no restaurants. The hills were dotted with sheep in the spring and summer, and the children played in the dirt or on poorly paved streets. Although they went to church on Sundays and believed in

God, the villagers were not a particularly devout people. If you picture a small, rural town in the hills of Tennessee, you will have a pretty accurate picture of life before 1981.

In the last ten years there have been some major changes. They have paved the main street, put in electric streetlights (which were never on while we were there), installed plumbing, and built many guest houses, cafes, and one hotel. None of the guest houses or the hotel has central heat or air, however. The rooms are very plain with two single beds, a dresser, and indoor/outdoor carpeting. There are quite a few cars for such a rural setting, but they still use carts drawn by donkeys to move hay or take in crops. There are more people living there now, although many of them are the younger villagers who left the area in order to get work in the cities and have returned. Perhaps the biggest change has been in the people themselves. They now go to Mass daily and recite the entire rosary as a village every evening. The old ladies with their worn faces, black coats, and babushkas; the young couples with their small children; and everyone in between come every day. They seem to consider it just a normal, routine part of the day. And all this in a church that has no heat or padded kneelers! My toes and fingers were actually numb from the cold some evenings.

The first full day in Medjugorje was Sunday the sixth, Epiphany. We went to the English-speaking Mass at noon at Saint James Church (they also celebrate liturgies every day in French, German, Italian, and Croatian). Although I did not realize it at the time, the homily at this liturgy provided the answer for why I had traveled all these many miles. The priest talked about the gifts of the three wise men to the infant Jesus. He said that in the same way we should be open to receiving the gifts of God. "Why wouldn't we be?" I thought. Because, he continued as if he had read my thoughts, when someone gives us very special gifts (material items or acceptance, friendship, love), the act of giving can draw us into an intimacy with the giver. An intimate relationship with another, even God, requires vulnerability. Often we are afraid of that vulnerability. We are afraid of what that might cost us; of what might be expected of us. And so, even if we long for the experience of being at one with each other and with our God, we can, out of fear, do or say all kinds of things that prevent that relationship from happening. Reflecting on the homily that evening, I wrote in my journal that I felt I was open to any experience here in Medjugorje. However, the truth hidden deep in my soul was that I was not.

The next day at the English morning mass I was quite startled to hear myself say at the end of the consecration, "Lord, I am not *ready* to receive you," instead of the correct words, "Lord, I am not *worthy* to receive you." So stunned was I at this Freudian slip that I never finished the sentence, "but only say the words and I shall be healed." When I finally said them to myself a few minutes later, it was with a deep emotional commitment to my faith that this healing could occur if I was willing to allow it.

This slip also opened me up to the realization that I did have my own agenda for this pilgrimage. I had come with the idea that God was going to tell me or show me what he wanted me to do for the future. Now that I had completed my degree in pastoral counseling, I questioned whether just being a pastoral counselor was "enough." Was I being called to an even greater service that had pastoral counseling as its base? In short, I wanted to know what else God expected of me as one of his followers.

I do believe that God gives to me. I even believe that I deserve it. I have had many wonderful experiences of God's loving presence in my life. And I really am very happy to give, to show my love for my God by serving others. I have been blessed with many gifts. It feels right to pass them on. Yet when I came to this special place in the mountains of Yugoslavia, I came prepared only to give, to serve—not to be given to. God in his infinite wisdom knew this, and instead of giving me what I wanted, he gave me what I needed.

I spent the next six days in Medjugorje as the receiver of gifts. It felt wonderful and at the same time somewhat awkward. I caught myself wondering how I was going to reciprocate. What could I do in return? Gradually, it occurred to me that just being the fullness of who God created me to be might be enough. If I wanted to pass these gifts on in other ways that would be nice, but it was not a condition for the giving. How freeing that was for me!

As wonderful and healing as this particular insight was, it was only the beginning. Over the next six days I had many things happen of which I am still seeing the effects in my life today. There were healing experiences having to do with the time I was attacked by a group of boys when I was seven years old. There was the wonderful vision of an entire village of normal, everyday people who are living together in unity and peace without sacrificing their individuality. And I had the experience of visiting with two of the visionaries and wondering at their humble acceptance of their special role in salvation history. They were very ordinary, very human. They did not walk around acting more pious and holy than the pope, nor did they presume to be more special than anyone else. For reasons neither they nor the village understood, Mary had chosen to come to them so she could deliver messages for the spiritual benefit of all people. The visionaries stressed the importance of her messages. They patiently answered the common questions (what does she look like? can you touch her? what is her favorite song? and so on), and were gentle with the people who needed to touch them (sometimes not so gently), but you could see by their facial expressions and body language that it was all a bit wearing on them. Sometimes they would become frustrated and gently scold the crowds about their need for the mundane details being greater than their desire to hear the messages of peace and love, but on the whole they were understanding of our human frailty.

It was a gift for me to see the extraordinary in the presence of the ordinary. I come from two religious traditions that put a lot of emphasis on the people who played a role in salvation history. However, by the time we Catholics/Episcopalians hear about them, their good qualities have become larger than life and their sometimes all-too-human qualities have been either lost or whitewashed to fit a certain theology. I needed to see that God calls simple, ordinary people like the visionaries, and like you and me, Catholic and non-Catholic, to respond to the challenge of becoming each in our own unique way the incarnation of his/her presence.

Mary provides a good example of what I mean by elevating the ordinary person to a position of such extraordinariness that all humanity is lost. Frequently in my past church experiences

Mary has been lifted up as a young girl who never felt moments of doubt, confusion, dread, fear, anxiety, sexual desire, loneliness, anger, or physical discomfort. The holy fathers of these churches have limited her feelings to great joy and deep sadness. For me this diminishes her rich complexity and devalues her faith commitment.

Mary's extraordinariness, like the visionaries', lies in the fact that even in the face of difficult circumstances she did not take back her assertive yes to God. Mary was one of us—very human, yet called to reveal the divine. She was a woman I can understand and relate to spiritually. She understands our struggles and provides a role model for the universal community.

When I was a child in Sunday school classes, I remember the teacher telling us about the Nicene Creed, part of which stated, "We believe in one holy catholic and apostolic Church." How, my eleven-year-old mind wondered, could we be Catholic when we were Episcopalians? "It means universal," my teacher explained. "Catholic with a little *c*," she said. I never forgot that. This was important to me because, as the child of a military officer, I had grown up with a very inclusive definition of community. Experientially I knew the meaning of *catholic* (universal), what the word *universal* meant. Because I knew, it was and is difficult for me to feel at home in a town, a church, or an institution that lives a narrow sense of identity.

When I chose to follow the Roman Catholic tradition as an adult, I did so in part because it seemed to attract people from all socio-economic levels. By their ethnic appearance and dress there appeared to be people from all walks of life at Mass. Unlike the English Catholics (Episcopalians), it looked to my eyes like a true universal gathering of all God's children.

Having been a professed Roman Catholic for eight years now, I realize that looks can be deceiving. Although it appears universal, the church supports doctrines and practices that exclude certain people. This lack of appreciation for the gifts of our rich diversity has divided the Roman Catholic Church into many bitter factions. Each one believes, of course, that it and it alone is the bearer of truth. The irony is that each faction is striving for unity and peace, yet many times the need to be right is more important than being one.

In Medjugorje I witnessed universality. There was a spirit of acceptance toward all people. During the Mass there was no verbal announcement or written notice in a bulletin about who may or may not participate in the eucharistic celebration. All who were spiritually hungry were invited to receive the bread of life. Watching people from all over the world and with different faith traditions come together in the breaking of the bread was like gaining a glimpse of the kingdom. No longer were we Catholics, Lutherans, Unitarians, Methodists, or Muslims, but simply the children of God wishing to physically, emotionally, and spiritually connect with our loving parent through the Son.

It was not perfect community living, of course. There were the pilgrims who frantically clutched at the visionaries and loudly proclaimed them to be Catholic saints. And there was the man behind me in the crowd outside a visionary's house who shouted that we should not forget that Mary was appearing to *Catholics*, when Ivan had just gently reminded us that Mary had come for the spiritual benefit of all people.

Many people asked questions of the visionaries that indicated they wanted their particular doctrine or their version of it to be validated by Mary. Yet over and over again, daily, hourly even, the villagers extended hospitality to everyone and the church authorities offered their acceptance to all, the reality of Mary's words. God calls us to be united in love and to live in peace. Medjugorje is not *for* Catholics with a big *C;* it is catholic with a little *c.*

Because of this emphasis there was great healing for me. At last I felt truly at home. Yes, they follow a Catholic ritual in Medjugorje, but the atmosphere is one of universal acceptance. All are welcome. Mary is the Mother of all and the queen of peace, and this tiny village in the mountains of Yugoslavia offers a glimpse of a world that follows her example. This catholic vision named and confirmed my deepest desires for global community. It was community in all of its ordinariness, but it was graced.

In *A Spirituality of Wholeness* by Bill Huebsch it is written:

> We are graced
> Everyone is graced
> Empowered, in other words,
> To move beyond and be transformed

The invitation of Medjugorje was to allow myself the gift of openness so that I might experience this transforming grace. God's constant revelation of himself in the ordinariness of the people, the universal acceptance of the church, and the gift of seeing and hearing how people might live with each other in peace was as powerful an experience of grace as any physical miracle that occurred there.

That God did communicate and does communicate with this world is something I have always believed. My God is a living God who makes his/her presence known in my life. So it did not come as a total surprise that I did experience some "spiritual phenomena." For those of you who have read or heard about such things, let me say that, yes, I did see the sun "dance" and no, my rosary beads did not turn gold, nor did I see the Blessed Mother. However, I did smell roses where there were no roses. The first time was while we were praying as we climbed the mountain of the cross, Mount Krizevac, and the second time was the same day in the church as we prayed the rosary that evening. I had not read about this particular experience, but after it happened the second time, I asked a woman in our group who had previously been to Medjugorje about it. She said that it has been known to happen to some pilgrims, although it is a less common phenomenon.

An important part of the journey for me was having the humility to accept that I needed to be with people who had experienced in a tangible way the sacred dimension. I said that I did not need to have the experience myself. I only needed to be in a place where it was said to be happening. However, even that, as I realized later, was a lie. Smelling the roses was a personal experience of the spirit world that touched me deeply. Like the poorest of the poor in spirit, I needed to have physical proof that God really did love me in a very intimate, personal way. Before that moment I did have faith and I did believe, but I denied that I was "one of those poor souls," as I referred to them, who hungered for the intimate touch of our loving God. Until I went to Medjugorje, my intellectual pride and my fear of such a special gift kept me from fully experiencing the divine in heart, mind, *and* body.

My pilgrimage to Medjugorje was frightening, humbling, and renewing. It helped me to integrate the separate streams of my life. The physical, emotional, spiritual, and sexual have now braided into a river. There is a greater wholeness, a stronger sense of who I am, and a deeper centering in God. As my river of life flows on in its journey toward heaven, I will be guided and nourished by the vision of a village that lives in catholic peace and unity, even as it is surrounded by hatred and war. The goal is to love ourselves, others, and God and to show this love as we go about the ordinariness of our daily lives. Medjugorje provided a truly catholic vision for my life as a Catholic.

T *he Madonna always stresses that there
is but one God and that people have
enforced unnatural separations. One cannot
truly believe, be a true Christian, if he does
not respect other religions as well. You do not
really believe in God if you make fun of other
religions.*

— Mirjana Dragicevic
  Conversation with Father Tomislav Vlasic
  Medjugorje, January 10, 1983

United Church of Christ: A Congregationalist's Perspective of Medjugorje

Priscilla Way

W ayne Weible's book, *Medjugorje: The Message,* lay around my house for weeks before I picked it up and read it. I had received the copy from my friend, Christine Kelly, who had read it upon the urging of her twin sister, Mary Hamilton. Mary had been to Medjugorje in August 1989 and was planning a return trip while hoping to take Christine with her. Christine gently reminded me several times to read the book, and, finally, when I did read it, I thought, "Wow, this is dynamite, and it is happening in our own time!" Wayne's book encouraged me. First, Wayne Weible is Lutheran, not Catholic, and that fact strongly affected me because I knew that Protestants as well as Catholics would read it and feel called (smart lady, our Blessed Mother). Second, I found the courage to pray "God, Thy will be done. If you want me to go to Medjugorje, please work it out." Thus I was able to let go of the need to try to make it happen. Finally, I started praying the rosary. Mary says the rosary is for all people and I felt that if I could help the world by praying this special prayer, then I would do it. It is a large time commitment every day, but it is one that has brought me much closer to God. Many of us forget about God or we do not put him first in our lives, tending to pray only when we have problems. Praying the rosary places God in a prominent place every day of my life, whether the day is joy filled or problem riddled.

Two months after reading Wayne's book, I spent a day with Mary Hamilton, something I rarely am able to do. When she invited me to go with her and Christine to Medjugorje, I was numb! My prayer had been answered. I must be careful what I ask for. I then began a crash course, reading everything I could on the subject.

My main reason for going on the trip was to pay homage to God and Mary. At the time, I felt something special was happening in Medjugorje, and it is happening right now, and I could be part of it. It seemed important for me that I make this pilgrimage. I expected somehow to find myself in the presence of the holy, and I was not disappointed.

Perhaps my pilgrimage to Medjugorje did not begin with Wayne Weible's book because, despite my Protestant upbringing, I have taken special notice of Mary for years and realized that without her we would not have Jesus. I probably first became aware of Mary years ago when I attended Mass with a friend at Cape Cod in the summer and noticed the statue of Mary in the church. I also saw her at the Basilica of Guadalupe in Mexico City and heard the story of how she appeared to a poor peasant. Later, when my mother was sick for many months before her death, I prayed that Mary would look over her and comfort her. Perhaps because I was fortunate enough to have a wonderful mother, I felt the gentleness of Mary and looked to her as the mother of us all. To me Mary is like an eternal mothering force, whereas I look to God as the Father. I feel I owe Mary something for looking after my mother when she was ill. I feel the same way about God: I feel the need to pray to him and praise him every day for all he has given to me.

I became part of a group of sixty-two from "Medjugorje Messengers," with Sister Margaret Catherine Sims as our leader. We flew to Zurich, Switzerland, on a Pan Am jumbo jet and then on to Yugoslavia. That country is the best kept secret in the world! Its beauty is revealed in mountains, hundreds of islands along the crystal blue Adriatic Sea, and small quaint towns scattered throughout the countryside.

If I could explain the whole experience in one word I'd say "awesome." I must confess, I did hope my rosary beads would turn to the golden color so I could return home and say to my skeptical friends, "See, now believe!" and also because I would have something concrete to show the doubting Thomases. But, of course, they did not turn.

Medjugorje brings people together from all over the world. These people all have one common bond—they believe in God. I loved celebrating Mass with all of them. At the Croatian mass only the natives could understand the language, but we all understood the singing of "Alleluia" and "Ave Maria." We were called the "pilgrims," and there was a special spirit among us of kindness and of helping each other that was reflective of the generosity of the peasants.

I had many beautiful personal experiences. It was as if I received special graces that opened my eyes and heart to see and appreciate all that was around me. I observed the dedication of the overworked Yugoslavian priests trying to minister to the throngs of people each day. I learned that confession was extremely important and meaningful to the Roman Catholics. Priests, who came as pilgrims from all over the world, would put up a sign near their chairs stating the language they spoke and then hear confessions for hours in that language. Many of the pilgrims had not been to confession in years. As a Protestant I was curious about this private confession experience, so after much thought and prayer, I went. An Irish priest (with a brogue) was so surprised when I told him I was a Congregationalist! Emerging from this unique experience, I felt a cleansing of my soul.

One of the spiritual manifestations that many pilgrims experience is the "miracle of the sun." I, too, was able to look directly at the sun without any damage to my eyes, and it appeared as if the Eucharist was in front of it. At other times a purple haze appeared around the sun. One day Christine, Mary, and I stood looking into the sun, marveling at the unexplainable and Christine saw the Blessed Mother holding the baby Jesus. Even though neither Mary nor I had the same experience, the observation was special for Christine because she had said she was going to Medjugorje to see the Blessed Mother, and she did.

Father Jozo was the original priest in Medjugorje when the apparitions began, and at first he did not believe in the apparitions. After a miraculous experience he became convinced of the truth of the apparitions, and he was eventually imprisoned for one to one and a half years for allowing the apparitions to be held in the church. I feel that he is truly a man of God, and this feeling was reinforced when I had a vision as he was preparing Communion on the altar. When I looked up I saw a white halo over his head and over the heads of the other priests who were sitting on either side of him. I also felt a wave of serene peace come over me as if I was in the presence of God. It was an awesome experience. We were in church seven hours that day, but I would do it once a week if I had the chance, for it was wonderful and one of the most memorable events of the trip. At the end of the healing service Father Jozo blessed each of us individually. When he put his hand on the top of my head, I felt an electric charge enter my body. Several others at the service had the same experience, and many were "slain in the Spirit" that day. Those who experience this say that they feel a peace that envelops them and they fall backward safely into another's arms.

The village itself takes a person back in time, and it gave me the feeling of being in Bethlehem. The houses are white stucco with red tile roofs. Many have a barn attached to the house where a cow and chickens reside. Grapes and vineyards are abundant, and some houses have an adjoining courtyard with grape vines overhead. We visited the home of the inner locutioners (two girls who receive auditory messages from Mary). We also visited two of the visionaries—Maria and Ivan. The visionaries receive petitions from the people and take them to Mary when there is an apparition. Some friends from home, knowing this process, gave us their petitions to take with us to give to the visionaries. Even though I was skeptical of this tradition, I handed in my petition of five requests when we went to visit Ivan. He took them to the apparition that night. When I awoke Sunday morning, I "got the feeling" to pray for one of my requests. I was amazed at the strength of the feeling. In fact I am still praying for that request. I realize I must be patient, and sometimes it takes years for things to work the way we would like them to work, if they ever do. God's timetable is not always ours.

Mount Krizevac's terrain is very rocky and difficult to climb. Since I had a hard time climbing down Apparition Hill, Christine's sister, Mary, told me I would never make it up the "big hill." I dutifully accepted her pronouncement and decided I would sit at the second Station of the Cross and wait there until everyone returned. The morning of the climb a feeling of great sadness came over me. All of a sudden I realized the Blessed Mother wanted me to climb up that mountain, and so I decided to try. Halfway up the mountain, one of the men in our group came over, silently took my hand, led me up to the top, and carefully helped me down (while his wife navigated the rocks like a mountain goat next to us!). That experience signified to me one of the many unspoken happenings of Mary working through others in Medjugorje and around the world. The view from the top of the mountain was magnificent. You could see a panoramic view for miles and observe several towns below. There is a huge cross at the top that the people of the town built in 1933 to commemorate the nineteen hundredth anniversary of the death of Jesus on the cross. There is no road, no electricity, no water, and no easy way for the people in the villages below the mountain to bring up the cement they needed to build the large cross at the top. However, the villagers carried what they needed to the top of the mountain and built the cross.

Another day, six of us were walking along the road up into the hills to visit a village family. As we walked along, a car drove by us, and the dust from the side of the road swirled upward. Usually stirred-up dust would drop back down to the ground, but this dust rose thirty feet and swirled into a shape like a cyclone. I had never observed anything like it, so I stopped and watched. Then the cyclone shape eventually opened up into the figure of Mary with a veil flowing from her head. She was wearing a long gown with a belt at the waist. I thought, "Well, I have experienced a lot here, but am not going to mention this, or my friends will think that I have gone completely mad." My fears were calmed when someone else in our party turned and said, "Did you see that!" Three of us had observed her!

Medjugorje helped me to realize that I need to live my faith every day by remembering God, putting him first in my life, praying, fasting, and attending church regularly. I do not profess to be perfect in all these areas, but I am trying. I was baptized a Methodist, confirmed as a Baptist, and attended the Presbyterian Church grades eight through twelve, also singing in the choir. I married a Presbyterian in his church, and then, when we moved to New England, there were few Methodist and Presbyterian churches in our area, so we joined the Congregational Church. My minister, Reverend Leonard Warner, has been with our congregation for over seventeen years, and he has been most helpful in leading me on my spiritual journey. I look at our church and its members as an extended family. I try to continue learning whenever we have a Bible study, video/discussion group, a special lenten series, or our once-a-year retreat. I joined a prayer group and have taken a "Life in the Spirit" course at our local Catholic church. Upon returning from my trip I began speaking to many people about my experiences. A friend had a gathering for twenty-two of her Catholic friends, and I spent an hour telling them of my experiences. Now that is what I call a captive audience! I have purchased and passed out over sixty of Wayne Weible's books, and when a book is returned, I pass it on for another to read. I feel great joy when people tell me they have purchased the book for themselves (one of my Protestant friends has purchased twenty-six) or when they say to me that after reading the book they now say the rosary. I hope to make a life commitment of telling people who are willing to listen about Medjugorje. My life will never be the same. We who have gone feel we were part of something very special, and we want to share.

As I came away I had a tremendous sense of Mary bringing us closer to God. After being there, I would repeat: It is a special place where there are special graces. In days of old, people went on crusades to the Holy Land. Today there are many "holy" places all over the world, and Medjugorje is one of them. I feel closer to God since my return, and I try to remember him in adoration. I feel going to church is a way of praising God and honoring him. I think about God in a much more serious manner and try to learn more all the time. I try to appreciate the small things in life: a smile, a flower, and especially my family and friends. Each day I ask God if I may be an instrument for him. I learned a prayer that I love. It is the one the angel told the three children he visited at Fatima. He said, "Oh God, I believe, I adore, I trust, and I love you, and I implore a pardon for all those who do not believe, do not adore, do not trust, or do not love you." I feel Mary is calling all of us to believe, adore, trust, love, and pardon, and thus she is leading us to God. She is the great mother of all of us, and she acts as a beautiful mother to Jesus as well as to us. I often think how different life would be if she had said no to the angel when he came to tell her of this unusual birth. Mary is now trying to be our Mother, help us to find God, and teach us to put him first in our lives.

On June 25, 1991, the tenth anniversary of the apparitions, Mary said: "Dear children: Today on this great day that you have given to me, I desire to bless all of you and to say, 'These days while I am with you are days of grace. I desire to teach you and to help you walk on the path to holiness.' There are many people who do not desire to understand my messages and to accept with seriousness what I am saying. But you are therefore called and asked that by your lives and your daily living you witness my presence. If you pray, God will help you discover the true reason for my coming. Therefore, little children, pray and read the sacred Scripture, so that through my coming you discover the message in sacred Scripture for you."

I would like to share one experience I had after I returned from Medjugorje. I had a health problem, and when I finally made a doctor's appointment I was told I would need tests, because a solid tumor mass was discovered on my uterus. After surgery I was told that in 80 percent of women with this type of tumor, it is found to be cancerous. Six weeks before the operation two friends handed me two different books on angels to read. Being a Protestant, I have never given much thought to angels in my life, but my interest was piqued, so I read both books. On the morning of my operation, I was in my bedroom getting ready to leave for the hospital, when the "thought" came into my head to stop and listen. I could see two clouds parting and knew someone was standing behind the left cloud, and way far away I heard a group of fifteen to twenty angels singing and I knew they were singing to me. What a beautiful gift from God. I was at peace and well prepared for the outcome of the operation. My tumor was not cancerous, thank God.

My minister, Reverend Leonard Warner, read my views on Medjugorje and discussed the Congregationalist's point of view theologically. He said the United Church of Christ (UCC) is *not* a doctrinal church, so it has no stand on Mary. In general, we believe God is present to us directly and not through an intermediary. Thus, anything that appears to mediate God's message is suspect to most Congregationalists. The idea of angels and apparitions is strange to the UCC. We believe the Holy Spirit works in and the through us, and some people have special revelations for the good of all people. In discussing Mary, Reverend Warner said: "Mary invites you to God—*not* to look at her—look beyond Mary—as though she were the window you do not see—to the view of what is God beyond." In fact, through her messages, Mary has said exactly that to us.

I love my church and the simplicity of it, of talking directly to God and seeing him work through our members. I feel I am strong in my faith and have drawn closer to God. We must be open to him, to love him and honor him. My church allowed me to go with an open mind, where I could have freedom and joy and make my own choices. The UCC allows for individuality as one evolves as a Christian.

Medjugorje helped me to understand more about other religions. Mary says there is only one God and we are the ones who have split the pie into many pieces with different religions. She says we are to respect other religions. I believe Mary comes through the Catholic religion because they believe in her, but that she has a message for all of us.

I do believe God knows each and every one of us and looks into our hearts to see the love we give and how kind and good we are to our fellow human beings.

Since writing this article about my experience of Medjugorje, I have had a tragedy occur in my family. My oldest son, Jonathan, and his wife, Elizabeth, had a beautiful baby girl, Erica Grace, who was born with many problems. She had a broken leg that has healed, she has club feet that can be corrected through surgery, but in the womb in the sixth month something happened that deadened the nerves at the bottom of her spine and she has no feeling in her legs, so she will never walk. We all take life and our physical body for granted until something like this makes us realize that each of us is a miracle. I pray for Jon, Liz, and Erica and feel we all need God and his love and support more than ever.

I *am calling you to a complete surrender to
God. Let everything that you possess be in
the hands of God. Only in that way shall you
have joy in your heart. Little children, rejoice
in everything that you have. Give thanks to
God because everything is God's gift to you.
That way in your life you shall be able to give
thanks for everything and discover God in
everything, even in the smallest flower. Thank
you for your response to my call.*

—Message given to visionaries by Mary,
April 25, 1989

A Baptist's Experience in Medjugorje

Victoria A. Foshey

T he messages of our Lady of Medjugorje have made a
great impact on my life. Most people who believe in the
apparitions that have occurred since 1981 are Roman Catholic.
Yet there are a number of people from different denominations of Christianity and other religions who have taken to
their hearts the events in Medjugorje. I am one of those people. However, my belief in apparitions and in the Virgin Mary
did not start with Medjugorje, but have been an ongoing
interest and conviction since I was a child.

I am not sure when I first became aware of the existence of
God. My earliest memory of God occurred when I was five
years old at Christmastime. My parents taught me the story of
Christmas, and I was so impressed by it that I never got tired
of hearing it. In fact, I asked for a figurine of the Madonna of
the Streets for my Christmas present that year. That same
Christmas my grandparents gave me a nativity set that I had
admired at a local department store. I still have this keepsake,
which always brings back fond memories of Christmas past, of
my love of God, and of my grandfather who died two months
later. When I was seven, I had my first memorable experience
in a church. My grandfather had passed away, and my
mother's family had the funeral services at Saint Joseph's
Church. I remember all the majesty of the High Mass and
how the ceremony was so mysterious.

My parents raised our family in the Protestant Baptist faith,
which did not have a mysterious or ceremonial quality. It is a
simple, straightforward type of faith. My parents did not
attend church regularly because they felt that God was everywhere and he could be prayed to and worshipped at any time
and at any place. However, we always attended church on

Palm Sunday and Easter, and I always looked forward to going. During the Easter season, I would watch all the religious specials like the story of *The Ten Commandments, The Greatest Story Ever Told, Ben Hur, The Robe,* and *Jesus of Nazareth.* All of these stories helped to contribute to my knowledge of God, Jesus, and the Bible. At this time, my parents purchased a children's Bible, which I still have. I read this book continuously in my need to know more about God.

During this time, I came to a better realization of who the Virgin Mary was. The reading of the Bible and the movies I had seen gave me a more complete picture of Mary and her importance. My love for her had grown since I first heard about her in the story of the Nativity. Mary was starting to take a vital role in my life, and it had a snowballing effect. Seeing the movie *The Song of Bernadette* one Easter when I was ten years old began a spiritual ball rolling. The movie so piqued my interest that I tried to read everything I could find concerning our Lady of Lourdes and Saint Bernadette. From there I started to wear a Miraculous Medal of the Virgin Mary and continued to learn more about our Lady and her apparitions. My love of our Lady would continue throughout my childhood until today.

Our Lady has had a great impact on my life. First, she provided me with the perfect role model as a Christian and a woman. Second, Mary showed me what is good and worthwhile in a world that is plagued with doubt and cruelty. It is easy to become disillusioned with a world that has lost its values, and it is not difficult to become confused about what is right and wrong. However, Mary leads us to Jesus, who clearly shows us what is *right* and *important* in the world.

It may seem confusing that a Baptist Protestant would have such a devotion to the Blessed Virgin Mary. However, I do not believe that the two should be incompatible when considering Scripture. In the Protestant faith, Mary is barely mentioned except at Christmastime. Her significance is relegated to giving birth to Jesus. However, we as human beings give significance to our mothers for helping us to become who we are. We do not diminish their importance to just giving birth to us. Should we do less for Jesus' mother? Not only is this attitude disrespectful of Mary, but I believe it is also disrespectful to

Jesus. Would Jesus want us to treat his mother as only someone who gave birth to him? When Jesus was dying on the cross, one of his last thoughts was to tell his disciple John that he should look to Mary as his mother. She played a role in the beginning of Jesus' ministry at Cana and after at the birth of the church. She also played a vital role with the Disciples during the day of the Pentecost. When considering these points, should not all Christians give more importance to Mary?

As a Protestant, I am aware of the fear we have about the Catholic Church's so-called worship of Mary. Most of these impressions are not founded on fact but instead on misunderstandings of Catholic teachings. In fact, most of the impressions that Protestants have of Catholics are superficial and lacking in true knowledge of what the Catholic Church is all about. There are many similarities between the Protestant and the Catholic faiths. If people were more open to other faiths, they might realize that the differences are not so great. As Christians, we all worship the same God and revere Jesus as our savior. We need to put our differences behind us and concentrate on the similarities while still respecting the differences. It is respect and love that Jesus showed to us during his lifetime. It is by following his example of showing love and respect to all that we show our love of Jesus.

It is through Jesus that I first learned about Mary, and through Mary I learned more about Jesus. All of Mary's recognized apparitions call us to follow her son, Jesus. The first apparition I learned about was Lourdes. As time went on, I learned about the apparitions of Fatima, LaSalette, and Knock, and Mary's visitation to Saint Catherine Laboure in Paris, France. The apparitions had a special effect on me, but it was not because of the supernatural miracles. What touched my heart was Mary's maternal special caring and love as she helps us to find God's love and happiness. When I first heard about Medjugorje one and half years ago, it had the same impact on me that the other apparitions had. I never knew that a story I would hear at a Saint Patrick's Day party would have such an impact in my life. As a child, I dreamed of what it must have been like to live and take part in the miracles of Lourdes and Fatima. I never dreamed that I would someday be able to visit a modern day Lourdes or Fatima.

On Saint Patrick's Day 1990, I heard my friend's mother speak about a town in Yugoslavia called Medjugorje. She told me of six children who had been seeing the Virgin Mary for a few years. My friend's mother is an Irish Catholic, and she mentioned the story because she had overheard me speak about Lourdes to someone. I had never heard about Medjugorje, so I was very interested. However, it was not until September that I heard about Medjugorje again. I had just started a new job, and some of the employees were talking about people who had been there. The more I heard, the more I became interested. However, it was not until Christmas when I saw my friend's mother again that I decided to visit Medjugorje. The one thing that I realized right away was that deciding to go to Medjugorje was easy, but getting there was not. First, I decided to do some research. I ordered a videotape and two books. After reading the books, I started to hunt for a tour that would be going to Medjugorje. The hunt turned into a wild goose chase. I called local churches, they told me to call the local Catholic newspaper, and the local newspaper told me to call the diocese in my area. However, the local diocese was less than helpful. They told me that the Catholic Church did not recognize the apparitions of Medjugorje yet, and the conversation ended abruptly.

Eventually, after a few weeks of searching for a pilgrimage, my boss told me of a nun who arranged pilgrimages to Medjugorje. I called her and received literature about a pilgrimage leaving during Holy Week, which excited me because of the thought of going during a holy celebration. I arranged for the time off at work and sent in my one hundred dollar deposit. I thought that the trip was set; however, I had no idea of the many obstacles we would have to face. A few weeks later I received a note from the sister telling me that she did not have enough people (ten were needed) signed up for the trip. The people who had signed up were backing out because of the Persian Gulf War. She mentioned that the trip would probably be canceled and rescheduled for the tenth anniversary of the apparitions, in June. However, I could not travel at that time because of my job. I was very disappointed but tried to turn the disappointment into something positive, so I decided to plan a trip to Lourdes. Unfortunately, this pilgrimage was also canceled because of the war. At this point, I was ready to give up the idea of going on any pilgrimages. However, the next week I heard again from the sister; she told me of another woman who wanted very much to go to Medjugorje. The sister said that if I would be interested in going to Medjugorje with the other woman, she would make all the necessary trip arrangements for us. At this time, a great unrest was beginning in Yugoslavia. My family and friends were concerned about me, and they wanted me to cancel the trip. I was very confused and began to wonder if I was meant to go. I prayed to God to let me know what I should do. I finally decided to go with the next available tour group.

The trip turned out to be a great adventure. All the challenges and confusion of the trip tested me and my faith. If you expect to travel to Medjugorje, you must expect trials of all kinds. It is as though the devil wants to rob you of the peace that God wants to give you. The sister told me to expect this, but I did not believe her until I lived the experience. The pilgrimage is a test, and you will discover this theme in the description of my trip. When you finally reach the goal of visiting Medjugorje, you feel an inner peace and thankfulness to God for seeing you through the journey.

Our journey started at Logan Airport in Boston, and then to JFK Airport, traveling on Yugoslavian Airlines, which we did not realize was on the verge of bankruptcy. The flight was smooth, but the plane itself did not seem to be in great shape. Since we were traveling on Good Friday, we had been fasting on bread and water. The concept of fasting is quite foreign to the Protestant faith, and it took a while for me to understand its purpose. Fasting helps you to control one of your most basic needs: food. When you can control your needs, it helps you to be more able to control your actions and desires. Fasting also helps reduce selfishness. On the plane, we started our novena to the Divine Mercy, which lasted nine days until the Sunday after Easter. This novena was originated in Poland by Sister Faustina. To our great surprise, they were also praying the novena in Medjugorje, which was held at Saint James Church at 3:00 P.M. After several connecting flights and an easy trip through customs, we took a three hour bus ride to Medjugorje. The sky was grey and it had just started to rain.

The trip along the Adriatic Sea was punctuated with beautiful scenery with an Old-World flavor. As we passed through the different villages, we knew we were in a place that was vastly different from America. It was as though time had had only a slight impact on the country. However, there were some signs of the Western world. Some areas had small shopping centers and malls, and there was a great deal of litter in other areas. I was surprised at this because most of Europe is very clean by American standards.

The anticipation was building on the last leg of the long trip. Those who had already been to Medjugorje prayed about what their new experiences would be this time. As for the rest of us who were new to Medjugorje, we prayed and thought about what Medjugorje would be like. As we made our final approach into town and saw the twin towers of Saint James Church looming in the distance, we all knew it would be an experience that none of us would forget.

We approached the town around 2:30 P.M. and were taken to the guest house. The homes in the area reminded me of the cinderblock houses in Florida. When we arrived, we were informed that our tour group had not reserved enough rooms for our group, so to help make room for everyone, I roomed with another girl my age in the linen room. We became good friends and shared many memorable moments together in Medjugorje. The accommodations were very stark, but appropriate, and it helped to remind us why we were there. This was a pilgrimage, not a vacation. It reflected the idea of poverty and simplicity, which showed me how lucky I was in my life in the United States. I believe these are some of the messages that Mary is trying to remind us. Focus on what is important, not earthly accommodations.

If you were to ask me what were the most memorable moments of the pilgrimage, I would list the following. The first memory is the night of Mary's visitation on Apparition Hill. I prayed for my grandfather who was close to death back in Florida—at the time I did not know I would never get to say goodbye to him. My grandmother called me when I got back from Medjugorje, and I told her to tell my grandfather that I loved him. He died the next day. My grandfather had suffered many strokes and also had cancer, which had spread through his body. He was asleep most of the time and not very coherent. I flew to Florida for the funeral. Upon arriving at my grandmother's, she told me about an incident that had happened the week before, while my parents were visiting. On the night before my parents left to go home, my grandfather was his old self. He seemed to remember everything that had occurred in his life. He talked all night with my parents and grandmother. He even held my grandmother's hand and told her that they had shared a wonderful life together. The following morning my parents left to go home, and that afternoon my grandfather slipped into a coma. He died a few days later. From the moment I heard about this story, I knew that this was a gift from God to my family. My family could not understand how he was able to make that temporary recovery. All I know is that the night he recovered was the same night I prayed on Apparition Hill to Mary during her visitation.

The second most memorable moment of Medjugorje was climbing Mount Krizevac on Easter night during a full moon. I had not planned to do this, but I felt compelled to do so when I saw a small cross near the foot of the mountain while on a walk through town. I decided to follow the trail with my friend. We would later realize that this trail was the back way up the mountain that the visionaries sometimes use. The way was steep and at times difficult to follow, especially at night. However, as we approached the top of the mountain the full moon rose in the sky to light our way. When we reached the top, the wind picked up, making it very difficult to walk, yet one candle continued to burn by itself. The large cross glowed in the moonlight. It was a perfect moment.

The third most memorable thing about Medjugorje is Saint James Church. I loved going at 3:00 P.M. for the Divine Mercy Novena, which was mesmerizing. The speech from Father Jozo was uplifting and provided insight into the messages of Mary. He is not an imposing, unreachable figure; he has a very human and simple quality that put me at ease and made him endearing. The main highlight for me in the church was Mary's daily visit during the nightly recitation of the rosary. The experience of Medjugorje and the people I met there have touched my life and heart. It is an experience I will remember for the rest of my life.

I have learned through Medjugorje that God is everywhere. Many of the pilgrims upon leaving Medjugorje seemed very sorry to leave and could not wait to return to the village. However, although I was very glad to have the experience of Medjugorje, I did not feel sorry about leaving. Places like Medjugorje, Fatima, Lasalette, and Lourdes unite God's children and provide people with tremendous hope and strengthened faith, but these are not the only places one can feel God's presence. Mary is trying to call us back to God, and she picked Medjugorje to reach that goal. However, she wants us to continue our faith back in our churches, in our homes, or wherever we may be in life, just as we would in Medjugorje, Fatima, LaSallette, or Lourdes. Mary wants us to love God because God loves us so much. If we look to Mary for assistance, she will lead us to him. If God could trust her with his only Son, why can we not trust her with ourselves?

I *am a mother, that is why I came.*
You must not fear, for I am here.

—Message given to visionaries by Mary,
October 25, 1985

A Southern Baptist's Perspective of Medjugorje

Nancy Meszaros

I was raised Southern Baptist, and that Protestant tradition has a very earthly view of the Virgin Mary. To us she is simply, and also beautifully, the Mother of Jesus. She is not given any special attention in our weekly worship, but in the Christmas and Easter seasons she is given special recognition for the part she played in bringing Jesus into our world and in his leaving our world.

I had assumed that all Christians viewed Mary in this way. It was not until I became a teenager and developed friendships with Catholic schoolmates that I realized the importance of the Virgin Mary in the Roman Catholic Church. I was enthralled with their view of this devout Jewish girl. My Catholic friends told me the story of some children's apparitions of Mary in Fatima, Portugal, and of the information which Mary had given the children which was then sent to the Pope in the form of letters. Then, in 1962, I saw a movie on television that depicted the story of Fatima, and my fascination with Mary and her appearance grew. As a result of the movie and my new information from my Catholic friends, I made up my mind that if a Marian apparition ever occurred during my lifetime, no matter where it was occurring, I would go there to experience the miracle myself.

Twenty-six years later my resolve would be tested. One night in 1988 I was watching ABC's *20/20* with Tom Jarriel, and he was reporting about a group of people from Alabama who had made a pilgrimage to Medjugorje, Yugoslavia. The program relayed the story of how six children (who are now adults) were seeing the Virgin Mary on a daily basis and receiving messages for the world. The similarity between Fatima and

Medjugorje stunned and called me all at the same time. I was struck how my earlier resolve to travel to the place where apparitions were occurring still had the power to draw me. I knew immediately that I had to go to Medjugorje but was not sure how to get there. I prayed.

Several months later I was sharing my desire to go to Medjugorje with a friend and co-worker, Ruth Von den Bosch. To my amazement, she told me that she had just booked the trip herself and that she was pretty sure that there was still space available on the same tour. How many more coincidences does one need! I booked the trip, too. Ruth told me that people who make the trip to Medjugorje receive a gift from the Blessed Mother and that I was sure to receive a special gift because I was not Catholic and was being called to go. She said that the gift may be physical or spiritual and that all I had to do was to be open. Ruth is a devout Catholic who had quit smoking several months before so that she would not have any trouble climbing Mount Krizevac. This dedication and renunciation also intrigued me.

Ruth and I shared a room in a Croatian home in the town. One night as I was returning to my bed from the bathroom I saw a large ball of light on the ceiling above Ruth's head. Ruth was sound asleep and I chose not to awaken her. The ball looked like a full moon on a hazy night. The center of the ball of light was brilliantly white and the light all around it was misty. It seemed to illuminate the entire room. My first thought was that my eyes could not focus properly after having been in the bathroom light, so I blinked my eyes several times, but the ball of light was still there exactly the same as before. My next thought was that perhaps it was early morning and the light was streaming in through the shutters. But the light was not streaming in through the shutters. It was not beams of light, but a ball of light. I again closed my eyes, this time a little longer. When I opened them the ball was still there. I was puzzled as to what this ball of light could be. There was no light anywhere in the darkened room, and the light was clearly not coming from outside the room. My eyes had by now adjusted to the dark, but the light was still there exactly as it appeared before my various attempts to find its source. I closed my eyes once again, much longer this time, and when I opened them this time the light was gone.

The next morning I told Ruth about my strange experience the night before while she slept. Ruth was sure that this was a gift to me from the Blessed Mother, and she wanted me to tell the priest who had accompanied us on our pilgrimage. I told her that I did not want to tell anyone, that I just wanted to think about it and pray about it. I was very tired that day, so I did not go with the other pilgrims to the scheduled events. Instead, I rested and walked around the village and contemplated my experience. When Ruth returned from the outing that afternoon, she was very excited. She told me that the villagers and pilgrims had seen the Blessed Mother in lights all over the countryside the previous night. Ruth was sure that I had seen her light as well.

After thinking and praying about my experience, I now believe that the light was supernatural in origin, but that the light was not for me but for Ruth. Since our trip in September of 1988, Ruth has written a children's coloring book of the story of Medjugorje and opened a religious book store. In addition, she has returned to Medjugorje every year since, except 1991 because of the Gulf War and the civil unrest.

As for myself, I do not feel saddened to think that the beautiful ball of light was not there for me but for Ruth. I had experienced much in Medjugorje and I feel truly blessed. One particular highlight that continues to give me comfort to this day is the trip to hear Father Jozo speak. His beautiful voice and holy presence made me feel very peaceful. I can still regain the feeling of calm when I think about him and remember the message he gave us. As a Baptist, I feel blessed for having made the trip and know that Mary is the Mother of all of us. Southern Baptists are taught to pray directly to Jesus without any intermediary. I now believe in praying to Mary. As the Mother of Jesus, she is able to amplify and redefine our prayers to Jesus, and our Father. My mother passed away with cancer in October of 1990. I am no longer able to feel her loving arms hug me, but when I pray to Mary, I feel, maybe imagine, Mary's arms around me, comforting me in my sadness and grief. She calls each of us to renew ourselves and our commitment to God whether we are Southern Baptist or Roman Catholic. I feel as strong as ever in my Southern Baptist religion, but more open to the Roman Catholic tradition and acceptance of Mary as our Blessed Spiritual Mother.

*D*ear children, today also I am inviting
you to a complete surrender to God.
*Dear children, you are not conscious of how
God loves you with such a great love, because
he permits me to be with you so I can instruct
you and help you to find the way of peace.
This way, however, you cannot discover if you
do not pray. Therefore, dear children, forsake
everything and consecrate your time to God
and then God will bestow gifts upon you and
bless you.*

—Message given to visionaries by Mary,
March 25, 1988

The Silence and Symphony of Medjugorje: An Episcopalian, Congregationalist, Roman Catholic Perspective

Janet Mendes

M edjugorje is like a Beethoven symphony. The power, beauty, and infiniteness of God resonate in the silence and the humbleness of the setting. And to those who hear the impassioned pleas of a mother crying in the wilderness for her children—God's children—it is like the sweet soothing fragrance of a rose. A rose of love that will heal the wounds of a world that so desperately cries for peace.

In Medjugorje the silent trumpets resound in this continuing, endless symphony of an ever-loving God who calls his people to salvation. "I am the voice of one crying in the wilderness 'Make straight the way of the Lord'" (John 1:23), said John the Baptist before the Savior arrived. And now Mary, the mother of this savior, our Lord Jesus Christ, comes to the world with the same cry for salvation. And she comes on the Feast of the birth of John the Baptist, June 24, 1981, to six children who hear her voice and come. They trust, they believe, they have faith—like all children. But the world lies sleeping—deaf, dumb, and blind to the children's cries and to its mother. The children are persecuted, but still the world sleeps on in disbelief. It was the same many years ago when a savior, a God made man, came to show his people how to live. He, like his Mother today, came in silence. Without fanfare, he was born in a manger. He came without crown or riches, so the world did not know him. Yes, "God chose what is foolish in the world to shame the wise, God chose what is weak in the world to shame the strong, God chose what is low and despised in the world, even things that are not, to bring to nothing things that are, so that no human being might boast in the presence of God" (I Corinthians 1:27).

Ah . . . our God, our Creator . . . so humble, so loving, simple and silent. And the world in its noise does not hear. Your majesty, your beauty, your voice is everywhere present . . . crying out in love for us. But we, being of the world, cannot see with the eyes of our souls. Our minds govern our soul. And our minds reflect the wisdom of the world. What cannot be discerned by knowledge and science is rejected. But you, God, who are the allness of love, cannot be dissected, qualified, or quantified. Like a Beethoven symphony, your love is the sweetness of sound resonating in silence . . . and it is this silence that will confound the wisdom of the wise!

The emptiness of words becomes apparent when describing Medjugorje. Perhaps that is why I have struggled and anguished over how best to share my thoughts and experiences. As a watercolorist and photographer, I would have preferred submitting a piece of artwork as an expression of the beauty and power of Medjugorje. For it is through art and music, not words, that the ineffable presence of God is felt. They are forms of prayer. And Medjugorje, more than anything else, is about prayer. Through prayer, says the Blessed Mother, anything is possible—even wars can be stopped, for "God governs the world, but prayer governs God" (*The Pieta Prayer Book*, 33). Only through prayer of the heart, and in particular, the prayer of the rosary, can peace be achieved:

> Dear children! Today also I am calling you to a complete surrender to God. You, dear children, are not conscious of how God loves you with such a great love. Because of it He permits me to be with you so I can instruct you and help you to find the way of peace. That way, however, you cannot discover if you do not pray. Therefore, dear children, God will bestow gifts upon you and bless you. Little children, do not forget that your life is fleeting like the spring flower which today is wondrously beautiful, but tomorrow has vanished. Therefore, pray in such a way that your prayer, your surrender to God, may become like a road sign. That way your witness will not only have

value for yourselves, but for all eternity. Thank you for having responded to my call.

This message was given by the Blessed Mother to the world through Mirjana, one of the visionaries in Yugoslavia, on March 25, 1988.

I first heard about Medjugorje through a friend—a normal, rational, sane-thinking friend who was raised Catholic but had been away from her faith for years. She went to Medjugorje in November 1990. She went as an interested, curious, yet skeptical pilgrim. And she returned home converted to God and renewed in her Catholic faith.

Intrigued by her experiences and filled with a desire to know more, I read *Medjugorje: The Message* by Wayne Weible and *Queen of the Cosmos* by Jan Connell. I was overwhelmed by what I read and was often moved to tears. My childhood Episcopalian faith had never prepared me for anything so powerful. Suddenly the distant God I had created in my mind was replaced by a real, live, loving Father—a Father who loves each and every one of us and is most intimately aware of our every thought, word, and deed. I learned that there are no coincidences in life, and that those often blessed accidents of fate are all orchestrated by God. And I learned about Mary. It is Mary whom Jesus turns to in his final agony of death and says, "Woman, behold thy son," and to John his beloved disciple, "Son, behold thy mother" (John 19:26, 27). At this significant moment of intense suffering and passion, Mary is asked by Jesus to make the supreme sacrifice of love—to forgive—to forgive humankind his death, and to become our Mother. It is as mother that Mary comes to Medjugorje with tears and urgent pleas to return to God. She is the messenger and it is through her that we, her children, come finally to her Son— and through her Son to our Father.

I was spiritual before Medjugorje, but not to the extent that I prayed or went to church with any consistency or regularity. My art was my prayer . . . my passion . . . my love. It was through art and the beauty of the world that I felt closest to God. Often when given a choice between a walk on the beach or going to church, I would choose the walk, preferring God's living world of art rather than man's version of God's art.

Churches, priests/ministers, people, and the hierarchical structure of the church often left me feeling spiritually empty and cold. And yet, as our two children grew out of toddlerhood, I was very aware of my desire that they receive some kind of formal, religious instruction. I frequented many churches of different faiths and finally found the Congregationalist faith to be the most comfortable for our family. This decision to embrace Congregationalism was based more on appearance than on substance. What most appealed to us about this faith, and the parish in particular, was the simplicity of the service, the dynamic manner in which the minister preached, and the family-oriented congregation. Out of obligation and responsibility, rather than true love and commitment to God, we resumed going to church.

Hearing about Medjugorje touched all the emotional chords of my soul. From the beginning I never had any doubt that what was happening in Medjugorje was real. I believed my friend; and the extensive reading that followed as a result of hearing about Medjugorje only confirmed my basic, intuitive trust. The scientific and personal documentation substantiating the supernatural miracles and wonders is voluminous, and the millions of pilgrims flocking to this holy mecca only further verified my sense of belief. Again the incredible simplicity and silence of God's hand at work conveyed the truth. I should also mention that at this time of deliberation and scrutiny into the extraordinary Medjugorje phenomena, I was greatly impressed by a friend's rosary. Not only had the silver links of the rosary changed to a golden color, but a face appeared on the originally faceless Jesus; the gap between the body of Christ and the crucifix was filled in by silver; and the crystal, clear rosary beads turned a luminous, iridescent color—a most impressive piece of confirming evidence which only further stimulated my desire to go to Medjugorje.

During the course of my insatiable reading and research, I learned about the rosary. This is the prayer that our Blessed Mother is asking all her children to pray. It is through the rosary, says our Blessed Mother, that the world will find peace. Having never heard of or seen a rosary before, I went to a Catholic bookstore and bought one. I also purchased a small how-to-pray-the-rosary book, so I could figure out what to do with my beads . . . and I began to pray. I cannot say that at the beginning I really had any idea or understanding of what I was praying. But I persisted, and slowly I began to appreciate what an incredible gift from heaven this powerful prayer is. The rosary is a prayer about the lives of Jesus and Mary; and it is a prayer from our Creator to show us, his creatures, how to live and what to value. On the surface it is a disarmingly simple and repetitive prayer, seemingly too simple to have much meaning, let alone capable of converting a world to peace. And yet underlying this deceivingly simple prayer lie layers and layers of truth which can only be discerned by praying the rosary daily. Like peeling the layers of skin off an onion, prayer of the rosary strips one's worldly self from the real self, so that we die to self and become one with God. The core of the onion is God, and the many layers of skin we peel off is our worldly armor.

My journal of May 1991 tells my story best.

I am finally on my way to Medjugorje. I go out of a deep sense of reverence for what God and our Blessed Mother have done for me . . . and are doing for all mankind. I go to give thanks, and I go for my husband, Peter, who has primary lateral sclerosis—a progressive neurological disease with no known cure—a disease that affects control of limbs and voluntary motor functions.

Although civil unrest is beginning to brew in Yugoslavia, I have no fear. By this time too many divine coincidences had occurred in my life, and I know that I am supposed to go. After thirteen hours of travel, our group arrives in Medjugorje. Our fatigue is intense but is immediately replaced by excitement and exhilaration at the newness of our surroundings. We go to church at Saint James to pray the rosary and participate in the Mass. I am seated between Italians on one side and Yugoslavians on the other. The church is filled. An electricity of emotion fills the air. God is present. Love, devotion, and deep gratitude reflect on all faces. I am overwhelmed. I cry and I cry and the tears keep coming. Tears of love, tears of joy, tears of sadness; I felt all kinds of tears during my week in Medjugorje. They were cleansing tears of my soul's aches. Amidst the humble surroundings is an undefinable presence of love . . . of beauty . . . of God. The visionaries we meet exude this presence. They have an interior grace and calm that reflects a heavenly peace. They answer our many questions with simplicity and love. Over and over, they tell us that the Blessed Mother asks us to pray the rosary, fast (a bodily form of prayer), convert to God, and have faith.

Perhaps my most moving experience is seeing Father Jozo. He was the parish priest at Medjugorje when the Blessed Mother first began appearing to the children. Father Jozo did not believe the children when they first told him of their visions. Then one evening during the praying of the rosary, the Blessed Mother appeared in the church and Father Jozo finally saw with his eyes what his soul had failed to see. Today Father Jozo is a man on fire. His intense passion and love are reflected in his every word and gesture. Often his eyes close when he speaks, and there is a stillness as though God is speaking. His words are spoken from the heart and they pierce the soul. The whisper and song of his voice convey the deep poetry of love within. At the end of the service, I consider asking Father Jozo if he will pray over me for Peter. I hesitate, wondering if this is an appropriate request and is within the rules of Catholic etiquette. In this moment's pause, Father Jozo turns to exit. He walks, maybe ten feet or more, and then, as if hearing the call of my heart, turns around and steps toward me. I am asked to kneel down. My eyes close and I feel Father Jozo's hands on my head. Words flow into a soft, soothing cadence of prayer. I weep. Tears of thanks moisten my face. I have been touched by the love of a living saint and I feel blessed.

Medjugorje is beautiful—quaint, picturesque, simple. Fields of brilliant red poppies dot the landscape along with fields of harvest. I am struck by the whiteness, fullness, and nearness of the clouds. The hills that surround us give an insulated, comforting feel. Birds abound and are constantly in song. The people mirror their landscape. There is a simplicity and beauty about them, along with a ruggedness reflecting years of hard work. I am glad to have my camera with me. Everywhere I turn, there is a picture. I hope, as I click away at cloud patterns, poppies, and people, that I may be one of those fortunate few to capture an extraordinary shot. Prior to my Medjugorje pilgrimage, a friend had given me a copy of a photograph taken on Podbrodo (Apparition) Hill of a tree. When the picture was developed, a very distinct image of the Blessed Mother was superimposed over the tree. I have seen other pictures that are equally sensational—pictures of roses with the face of the Blessed Mother in their centers and clouds that have formed into images of Christ. Aware of the potential of capturing a miraculous image, I spend a good part of my sojourn behind the lens of my camera, and in due time earn the nickname "Clicker." One of the most convincing outward manifestations that something remarkable is occurring is the phenomenon of the dancing sun. In typical photographer fashion, I take many pictures of the waltz in the sky, hoping that one will convince my skeptical friends back home of the veracity of the events taking place in Medjugorje. But again, Medjugorje is not about the externals—the spinning suns and signs—it's about prayer, peace, love, the Blessed Mother . . . and the Father. I wonder how I can photographically record what's happening to people interiorly. Perhaps my best hope is a picture I take of an old, old woman sitting intently by the side of a dirt road with rosary in hand; or the picture I take of a priest praying on Podbrodo Hill, a euphoric look of peace and serenity radiating on his face. Perhaps it's the silence of my pictures rather than the sensation that will touch hearts . . . and reveal the truth.

Our trip to Medjugorje is over before it is even begun. A week seems too short to absorb all the messages, miracles, and visions we experienced. If only we had had one extra week of quietness to reflect upon all the events. But alas, it is time to go. I wonder what to say to friends and family back home. They could not understand why I was going to Medjugorje in the first place. I wondered what words I could find to convince them that what is happening in Medjugorje is real and is for all of us. I thought to myself, if I were confined to a one-word testimonial on Medjugorje, I would raise the rosary and tell people to *pray.*

I am home now and my trip to Medjugorje seems like long ago. Peter's physical condition has worsened. Every step he takes is with effort. He occasionally falls. It is expected that the disease will spread, but so far Peter is able to continue working. I no longer have any anxiety about his illness. I know that what Peter has, he has for a reason, even if I do not understand. I know he is being watched over and loved. And I now know that my faith will carry me through the tomorrows.

Conversion to God has been joyous and at times painful. Medjugorje was the door of beginning on this road to conversion. I never realized how many holes and cobwebs had permeated my soul. As I became an adult, I lost being a child. I became "wise"; I forgot how to love; I became bogged down with appearances and preoccupied with self; I was critical and judgmental—especially with those nearest and dearest; and anxiety often consumed me. Yes, I was an adult. And to the world, I projected this image of a self in total control. I thought I was happy and at peace. It has taken Medjugorje and a lot of prayer to realize how unpeaceful I was. This intense, inward scrutiny of self is a part of the conversion process. Often the journey of personal transformation feels like being on a roller coaster of highs and lows. And so today, as I continue along this road of conversion to God, it is to my children I look to teach me how to be a child again. With God's grace, the child in me that has been suppressed by the adult will be released and set free . . . and I will die to self and be resurrected in Christ.

As of September 8, 1991, the Feast of the Blessed Mother's birthday, I have become a Catholic. I love going to Mass and I go daily. Receiving Jesus in the sacrament of the Holy Eucharist, Calvary relived, is the most treasured and sacred moment of my day: "The Mass is infinite like Jesus. It would be easier for the world to survive without the sun than to do without the Holy Mass," said Padre Pio, the stigmatic priest of Pietrelcina

(*Jesus Our Eucharistic Love* by Father Stefano Manelli, pp. 19–20). The Mass is truly the prayer of all prayers—the prayer of eternal light and sun. Listen to these words, as spoken by Mary April 25, 1988.

> Dear children! God wants to make you holy. Therefore, through me he is calling you to complete surrender. Let the holy Mass be your life. Understand that the church is God's palace, the place in which I gather you and want to show you the way to God. Come and pray.

If the Mass is the prayer of sunlight, the rosary is the prayer of moonlight that reflects and illuminates the powerful essence of the Eucharist. As I walk the journey of each day, it is the rosary I turn to for peace and strength. It is my steadfast friend and constant companion. Always I feel a deep sense of inner calm reverberate when I say and meditate upon its joyful, sorrowful, and glorious mysteries. I am eternally grateful and surprised by the new layers of meanings which surface from this prayer. It will be through this powerful prayer, through the cries and tears of a Mother who loves, through our God, our Jesus, that the world will be healed and we will be one. And so, the Beethoven symphony continues on a sustained note of silence . . . on a tear . . . on a note of prayer.

Epilogue

Sharon E. Cheston

I have prayed and pondered, what could I possibly add to the beautiful testimonial chapters that have been written so honestly and sincerely from the hearts of the authors? Perhaps it is interesting to note that when I have worked on edited works previously, it was like pulling taffy through a meat grinder to get authors to agree to write chapters and then to obtain the chapters promised by the deadline. This work has been nothing like those other experiences. Only one prospective author declined, and this happened only after she tried to commit the words to paper and felt she could not express fully the intense faith that she experienced in Medjugorje. "Words cannot express what I feel," she said.

On the contrary, all other writers commented on how easy it was to write the chapter. The authors experienced the writing as a gift to them, and many referred to it as a labor of love or an outpouring from within. Every person met the deadline and almost all chapters arrived weeks early.

As for myself, when I agreed to accept the project, I thought that I was crazy to try to squeeze in another obligation in an already overcommitted schedule. However, I felt that I had to do this. As I began to assemble the writers, I sensed urgency to complete the work but never said this to the writers until the last month. They worked independently as if they were on fire.

The sense of urgency has not abated now that I sit here and write the epilogue. The timing seems poignant. As I travel to speak to groups, I am struck with how informed Roman Catholics are about Medjugorje as compared with non-Roman Catholics. Perhaps it is because the Roman Catholic Church is hierarchical in its structure and is truly worldwide, while other faith groups are more independent of each other. The message from Medjugorje is very clear, though: Mary is the mother of all of us and she is calling *all* of us. So all of us must be made aware of what is occurring and what our response options are. Some of you will be called to travel to Medjugorje to experience the ambiance and blessed occurrences for yourselves. Others of you will not need to make the trip but will commit yourselves to reading and exploring the call of God through your own means. Still others of you may be skeptical and will want more proof. Whatever your response, I pray that God blesses and calls each and every reader and that you experience the importance and love of this call personally in your heart.

As this manuscript goes to press for the second time, the fighting in the former Yugoslavia continues. The horror and atrocities are being compared by the media to those committed under Hitler's regime. All sides of the war are accusing each other of the many wrongs committed. Trying to understand the complicated political, social, cultural, and religious underpinnings of the region seems impossible and each cease-fire fails, as if someone keeps stirring the pot enflamed by hatred. In the midst of this murky, seething caldron, Medjugorje fights to maintain its peaceful quality of life. As if Mary refuses to allow the war-filled destruction that surrounds the villages, bombs fall unexploded in the fields. One bomb was seen to fall directly toward Saint James, only to explode in midair before hitting the church. Yet only a few kilometers away Citluk was shelled beyond recognition. Mostar, Zagrab, and Dubrovnik—the major cities surrounding Medjugorje—have all been destroyed or heavily damaged.

The people of Medjugorje keep their faith fires burning, and as the war has moved away from Medjugorje and eastward toward Sarajevo, pilgrims are more frequent and refugees pour into the little town. During the siege, with fear escalating, little to eat, and poor utility conditions, Mary did not desert her villagers. She continued with daily Mass, prayer, and rosary. Who of us would not have been angry at God for allowing the war to continue, would not have doubted that our Lady of Medjugorje was still there with them, or would not have lost faith? But the people of Medjugorje did not desert God and did not discontinue their devotion.

This faith-filled tenacity is probably the greatest testimony of the reality of Mary's presence. The villagers believe that the power of prayer is the greatest weapon they have to diminish the foe and stop the war. They ask that you join them in the prayer for peace not only in Bosnia and the rest of the former Yugoslavia but also for all the people and countries around the world.

The monthly message given by Mary is received on the twenty-fifth of each month. In addition, Mary often gives messages to Ivan on Mondays and Fridays. If you are interested in learning more about the apparitions in Medjugorje and other apparitions around the world, I have listed centers that are dedicated to spreading our Blessed Mother's messages. A word of caution is necessary. These three centers are primarily organized and run by Roman Catholics. Therefore, the approach is understandably from the Roman Catholic tradition. However, the writing is accurate and devoted to informing all people of the apparitions. Look beyond the Roman Catholicism to the spirit of ecumenical catholicism. In addition, I will assist you in connecting with any of the authors of the chapters of this book if you wish to speak to them personally or if you wish to have a speaker address a group. We all feel blessed to have been given the opportunity to share our experiences with you, and we feel obligated as a result of having been called to Medjugorje to assist others in exploring their need for more information about this timely and important occurrence. Pray for us and we pledge to pray for each of you.

Medjugorje Information Centers

Caritas
Box 120
4647 Highway 280 East
Birmingham, AL 35242
Telephone: 205–672–2000

Newsletters
Prayer groups
Conferences
Our Mother's monthly
 messages in sixteen languages
Updates on war situation

Pilgrimages
Speakers
Rosaries
Video and audio tapes
Books

Medjugorje in America
P.O. Box 2200
Fitchburg, MA 01420
Telephone: 508–342–9250
FAX: 508–346–5058

Newsletters
Conferences

Speakers
Rosaries

Pittsburgh Center for Peace
6111 Steubenville Pike
McKees Rocks, PA 15136
Telephone: 412–787–9791

Major informative newspapers
Peace centers
Prayer groups

Newsletters
Monthly messages

References

Holy Bible, New King James Version. 1611. Nashville, Tennessee: Thomas Nelson, Inc.

Manelli, Stefano. *Jesus Our Eucharistic Love.* N.d. Brookings, South Dakota: Our Blessed Lady of Victory Mission.

Our Lady's Messages to the World. 1989. Framingham, Massachusetts: Medjugorje Messengers.

The Pieta Prayer Booklet. 1972. Hickory Corners, Michigan: Miraculous Lady of the Roses.

Two Friends of Medjugorje. 1990. *Words from Heaven.* Birmingham, Alabama: Saint James Publishing.

Valtorta, Maria. 1989. *Poem of the Man-God IV.* Isola del Lira, Italy: Centro Editorale Valtortiano Sr.

Weible, Wayne. 1985. *Miracle at Medjugorje Part 1: The Apparition.* Birmingham, Alabama: Caritas of Birmingham.

———. 1989. *Medjugorje: The Message.* New Orleans: Paraclete Press.

Contributors

William M. Ames is an entrepeneur and resides in Cambridge, Massachusetts. His company, Atlantic Financial Marketing, sells software to the banking industry.

Sharon E. Cheston, Ed.D., is a member of the Pastoral Counseling Department at Loyola College in Maryland. As a mental health practitioner, educator, and supervisor, Cheston has been teaching and supervising novice and experienced therapists in the art of counseling for more than seventeen years. Her private practice clientele consists primarily of clergy and mental health counselors. She is also a National Certified Counselor, a certified Mental Health Counselor, and a Certified Professional Counselor in Maryland.

Jane Culligan, S.C., M.A., M.S., A.D.T.R., is a New Jersey Sister of Charity holding master's degrees in education and counseling as well as postgraduate doctoral studies in creative arts. She is also a certified spiritual director, a registered dance therapist, and a liturgical dancer. Her background includes workshops, conferences, retreats on prayer, clinical supervisor in a New Jersey psychiatric hospital, and a year in residence with a Carmelite community in Australia and New Zealand.

Victoria A. Foshey is a secretary a Lawson-Hemphill, Inc., in Rhode Island. Her background includes an associate's degree in computer science and attendance at the University of Rhode Island. Her interests include reading, drawing, and sailing.

T. Joyce Lemmon is Owner/Administrator of Lemmon-Mitchell-Wiedefeld Funeral Home and Member of Maryland State and National Funeral Directors Associations. She is also a member of Cathedral of Mary Our Queen Medjugorje Rosary Group and Saint Joseph's Prayer Group. She was confirmed in the Catholic faith in April 1992.

Gay Lutton, R.N., M.S.N., M.S.: As a community health nurse and a pastoral counselor, Gay is working as the chaplain and bereavement coordinator for Children's National Medical Center Hospice Program, has a private practice in the Washington, D.C., area, and is active in the parish nursing movement.

Janet S. Mendes is a wife, mother of two, photographer, and artist. Her works have been shown at the Robert Klein Gallery in Boston, and she has been published in *Camera Arts, American Photographer, Outside Magazine,* and *Baby Talk.* Currently she is working on a watercolor series of abstract landscapes.

Nancy A. Meszaros is employed as a Divisions Clerk in the Inercarrier Revenues Department of a transportation company.

J. Steven Muse, Ph.D., is a Presbyterian minister and Fellow in the American Association of Pastoral Counselors. He is interested in the relationship between psychotherapy and Christian spirituality. His articles have appeared in *Journal of Pastoral Care* and *The Other Side,* and numerous essays have been published in *Monday Morning,* a magazine for Presbyterian ministers.

Christine Washburn is completing her master's degree in Pastoral Counseling at Loyola College in Maryland. She has been an active full-time church and community volunteer and has taught kindergarten and tennis for twelve years. Chrissy lives in Minneapolis with her husband and two children.

Priscilla J. Way, A.A.S., Keuka College, has been an Administrative Assistant for twelve years at Morrill Memorial Library, Norwood, Massachusetts. She is presently serving as Deaconess, First Congregational Church, and had previously served on the Christian Service Board (Mission and Out-Reach) and has acted as Chairperson. Priscilla aslo has served on the Church Council and Board of Deacons. She has been married for thirty-four years, is a mother of four, and is the grandmother of three.